THE ARTS THEATRE, LONDON
1927–1981

by Wendy and J.C. Trewin

1986
The Society for Theatre Research
London

ISBN 0 85430 041 4

Published by the Society for Theatre Research
77 Kinnerton Street, London SW1X 8ED

Printed in Great Britain by
E. & E. Plumridge Ltd., Linton, Cambridge

In Memory
of
Alec Clunes
1912–1970

FOREWORD

The English Arts Theatre Committee was formed by Alec Clunes as a play production and presentation company. In 1983, thirteen years after his death, it was decided to wind up the Company, and among a number of final commitments the Chairman, Frank Smith, and the Directors commissioned Wendy and J.C. Trewin to write a history of the Arts Theatre, London as a tribute to Alec Clunes. Mr. Trewin had already published a sympathetic biography of Alec Clunes during his lifetime.

The Society for Theatre Research was honoured to be offered a book by such distinguished theatre lovers and historians, and the Arts Theatre Committee also made a most generous grant towards its publication. Mr. Michael Warre and Miss Gillian Adams, two of the directors, gave invaluable help in locating and supplying illustrations.

The authors have borne with great patience and good humour the adaptation of their original script for publication by the Society. Theatre history, as a member of the Society pointed out at a meeting, is not just "something that happened a long time ago"; it is created daily. We are very pleased to have had the opportunity of publishing this record of perhaps London's most remarkable Twentieth Century "Little Theatre".

Kathleen Barker
Editor for the Society for Theatre Research

ACKNOWLEDGEMENTS

We are most grateful to all who have helped us during our research into the history of the Arts Theatre: in particular, the late Mr. Frank Smith, and the Directors of the English Arts Theatre Committee Ltd. – Miss Gillian Adams (Mrs. Jan Kurzke), Mr. John Allen, OBE, and Mr. Michael Warre – for their kindness over a long period; and Dr. Kathleen Barker, of the Society for Theatre Research, who has edited an intricate manuscript (twice the length originally) with unruffled skill and friendliness.

Our warm thanks also to Mrs. Daphne Clunes, Miss Jenny Laird, Mr. Christopher Fry, Mr. Nicholas Barter, Mr. William Wordsworth, the late Mr. John Fernald, and those from whom we have quoted.

W.E.T.
J.C.T.

Hampstead, 1985

CHAPTERS

CHAPTER ONE
FIRST ACT: 1927–1942

Today, in the 1980s, we are likely to run across a Fringe theatre almost anywhere in London, and in a wild variety of converted buildings, upper floors or basements, with no official grant and the smallest of audiences, sometimes a dozen people or fewer, more on the stage than in the auditorium. There have been occasional surprises, such as the year's run of a Fringe play, *Accidental Death of an Anarchist,* at so hallowed an address as Wyndham's; but these are surprising simply because they are so rare. The West End is oddly islanded, conscious of the companies that environ it and of a movement resolutely publicised, yet seldom joining in the fun itself.

During the mid–1920s the word 'Fringe' was unused; London had only a scatter of experimental, or club, theatres, principally in the suburbs and depending upon the infrequent transference of a play to the West End. The Everyman, up on the hill at Hampstead, and the weekly-change 'Q', Jack de Leon's generally commercial near-miracle at what had long been an all-purpose hall at Kew Bridge, were gallantly prolific on the outer bounds; in the West End we had to think, in unflinching avant-garde terms, of the Gate Theatre Studio which Peter Godfrey and his wife Molly Veness had founded in an attic above Floral Street, Covent Garden. (It would move to Villiers Street, Strand.) Producing societies (at one period they teemed like pilchards at St Ives) did their most fruitful work on Sunday nights, sometimes on Monday afternoons as well; the Stage Society was the most celebrated and the less formal Repertory Players the longest-lived. Actors and actresses, again and again frustrated in their most frustrating of careers, simply wished to act—where would be quite immaterial—and they seized any chances of a Sunday-night part, with perhaps a manager or two in front; after all, an overriding hope during the late Twenties, the play might go somewhere for a run.

All said, then, the West End had space enough in 1927 for a building that, according to its preliminary details, would combine the 'amenities of a London club and a congenial place for those interested in the theatre on both sides of the curtain'. Hence the foundation, for short runs and—who could prophesy?—possible transferences, of the Arts Theatre Club, designed by P. Morley Horder and splendidly accessible upon the north side of Great Newport Street, between Charing Cross Road and St Martin's Lane. Its first President, the honoured manager, Bronson Albery, was joint managing director of Wyndham Theatres Ltd, which controlled the late Sir Charles Wyndham's interest and that of the widow, Mary Moore. In a sense, the Arts could be a holiday for him, a relief from the inevitable single-mindedness of a family firm. Walter Payne, the Club chairman, was a prominent impresario in musical plays and variety; his deputy, W.E. Gillespie, had a similar background; Bernard Isaac and Lionel Barton were managing directors; and a long list of Vice-Presidents looked suitably impressive. Basil Dean, busiest and most feared of West End producers (the current term for director), whom Albery also wished to be a Vice-President, offered to put on later in 1927 Eugene O'Neill's still banned *Desire Under the Elms*. Though it was a good idea—for the Arts, as a club, had no trouble with the Censorship—Dean did not get the necessary finance, and the project died.

The Arts Theatre Club building, on the Salisbury Estate, cost £18,500. *The Times* described it as 'attractive' and, unexpectedly, as 'shaped somewhat like the House of Commons', not an analogy immediately obvious. Its basement theatre, holding then 324 people, had a workable if shallow stage, ready for most plays except the obstinately spectacular; in any event it was not a time for spectacle. Actually, the Arts had the smallest stage in Central London—slightly smaller even than the Gate's in Villiers Street—with a proscenium opening of under 21 feet and a height of 14½ feet. Cramped as it was (and so were the dressing-rooms) no one minded greatly. It could, and did, serve for an uncommon range of plays, presented sometimes by the Club itself; more often, at a 'reasonable charge,' by outside companies.

The Arts was lucky, too, in its restaurant and bars which the profession began at once to use freely; reading and writing-rooms, and a ballroom which sounded rather grandly superfluous. It opened on April 20, 1927, with *Picnic,* a revue originated by the Club, written mainly by Herbert Farjeon, already the wittiest man in his genre. Beverley Nichols wrote the music, Florence McHugh and Leslie French were in the cast, and the producer, Harold Scott, meant a lot to audiences who knew him as the prime mover, with Elsa Lanchester, in their Victorian cabaret in Seven Dials.

Once begun, the Arts programme would be diverse enough. St. John Ervine had written *The Lady of Belmont* as a satirical sequel to *The Merchant of Venice,* the kind of frolic in which Shylock (Brember Wills), now a Venetian Senator, and Portia (Barbara Everest) joined towards the end in amiable debate about the future of Jewry. Orthodox

Shakespearians were appalled; Ervine, kindest of Ulstermen but loving argument for its own sake, remained serene. Obviously this would not go to the wider West End, but two productions did, the more important John van Druten's *Young Woodley*, a gentle anecdote about a public schoolboy infatuated by his housemaster's wife. It had run steadily on Broadway: Basil Dean, trying to get the London ban raised—no producer worked harder at this sort of thing—had the support of the Three Hundred Club, conducted by Mrs. Geoffrey Whitworth (whose husband had founded the British Drama League) in association with the Stage Society. Bronson Albery at once offered the Arts; but because it was too small to hold all the Society's members, the première was on a Sunday night, down the road at Albery's New Theatre in St. Martin's Lane, with a week of Arts performances to follow. Lord Cromer, the Lord Chamberlain, came to one of these and raised the ban—'the first sign,' Dean said, 'of the loosening of the Chamberlain's ban on the English theatre'—and the play went on to its long life at the Savoy and several paragraphs in stage history. The second Arts transference, a first-anniversary production, was appropriately *Many Happy Returns,* another Farjeon revue, 'produced under the direction of Archibald de Bear,' and very soon removed to the Duke of York's with such people as Morris Harvey, Harold Scott, and Mimi Crawford, who sang 'I've danced with a man who's danced with a girl who's danced with the Prince of Wales'. It was a more enjoyable night than many in the year's list, a perplexing mixture. Certainly, at this remove, we can see no pressing reason for a comedy entitled *For First-Class Passengers Only,* written by Osbert and Sacheverell Sitwell, in which the three Sitwells appeared as themselves; or for pieces called *Flies and Treacle* and (a minor Milne) *Let's All Talk About Gerald.* Regular visitors—increasing week by week and content to take their chance—would have caught Edouard Bourdet's *La Prisonnière,* a study of a lesbian, prized in New York and transiently shocking; and two one-acters by Shaw, the grim little 'tragedietta', *A Glimpse of Reality,* that he wrote for Granville-Barker, and *The Fascinating Foundling*—'a disgrace to the author' he called it in 1909—that was graced by the young Peggy Ashcroft. We hear little now of Rupert Brooke's *Lithuania* or of George Moore's conceit, *The Making of an Immortal,* with Sybil Thorndike as Elizabeth, a regular royal queen, Charles Carson as Shakespeare, and Charles Laughton, regularly being 'discovered' about that time, as Ben Jonson.

The most important transfer of 1929 was Reginald Berkeley's *The Lady with a Lamp* which would be triumphant at the Garrick. Edith Evans, as concentrated as ever, created Florence Nightingale simply by insisting to herself that she was the woman—a quality of insistence few actresses had—impressing her belief upon the audience, and fixing mind and heart through the mutations of the chronicle. Here was a woman whom Ivor Brown, a critic as respected as any in his day, described[1] as 'half feminine and half administrative fanatic standing like an igneous rock among the waters of muddle and misrule'.

The Arts was justifying itself. Its list had room for, say, Claudel and Sudermann and Strindberg. Drama critics, accustomed by now to that dim auditorium, were not often alarmed by what might turn up, though they did admit a certain astonishment, early in 1930, at *The Humours of the Court* by the Poet Laureate, Robert Bridges. Edith Evans was in this, not among her remembered occasions; most of the actors belonged to the Oxford University Dramatic Society, produced by its President, Brewster Morgan, a thrustful young American, much admired locally though little else would be heard of him.

The Arts that year could offer plenty of names: John van Druten, with the restrained naturalism of *After All;* Benn Levy, with *The Devil,* aided by Sybil Thorndike and Norman McKinnel; and, remarkably, the young Alfred Tennyson. He was only fourteen when he wrote *The Devil and the Lady,* already with the feeling for vowel-sounds ('came sounding o'er the long Ionian'), and with those speeches for Magus—'the mighty waste of moaning waters' and so forth—that lead one irresistibly to the older poet. Shaw's *Jitta's Atonement,* the rarest of his plays in performance, was basically not his but a comedy by his Viennese translator, Siegfried Trebitsch, who could hardly have recognised the work when GBS had finished with it. Violet Vanbrugh acted the same part, Jitta, that she had created five years before at the Grand, Fulham, among the suburban theatres in final commission between the wars.

It was a season for linguists. During 1930 there were productions of Chlumberg's *Das Blaue von Himmel* in German; Racine's *Phèdre,* in French, with Sybil Thorndike, who never seemed to be tired; a play in Russian, staged by Theodore Komisarjevsky, whose reputation had mounted fast; Part One of *Faust,* in German; and *La Piccola,* in Italian, its two characters acted by Emlyn Williams and Betty Hardy, just contemplating a partnership in one of Williams' earliest plays, *Glamour.* Moreover, the Arts also did *A Doll's House* in English, with Gwen Ffrangcon-Davies as a Nora of delicate understanding, and Harcourt Williams—then in spate directing the Old Vic during the first of his fours years—as Dr. Rank. The autumn of 1930 began with George Moore's over-valued *The Passing of the Essenes;* and, in late November, Bruno Frank's comedy, *Sturm in Wasserglass* (in German) might have told any prophet—not many were around—that here one day would be James Bridie's *Storm in a Teacup.*

Any notes on the theatre at that time have to be a bran-tub dip. We can observe Edith Evans as the secretary to a fortunate Colonial

Governor in Reginald Berkeley's *O.H.M.S.;* a long way from *The Lady with a Lamp,* nothing more was heard of it except a token week at the New. Jean Forbes-Robertson played the Hedda Gabler she would repeat many years later; two rapid transfers were Ronald Mackenzie's *Musical Chairs,* with John Gielgud and Frank Vosper, to the Criterion, and (to the Prince of Wales') *Passing Through Lorraine*[2] by Lionel Hale, not long down from Oxford and among the most promising men of his generation. John Fernald, the producer, had known Hale's brother at Oxford; he and Lionel enjoyed themselves during the transfer when they substituted at matinees for two actors unable to appear.

Most especially, 1931 brought to the Arts Le Théâtre du Vieux Colombier (later La Compagnie des Quinze) before it moved up to the Ambassadors: first with Obey's *Noé,* 'like a poem by Blake', according to James Agate in *The Sunday Times*[3], 'acted by figures in a Gauguin canvas come to life, and talking the everyday jargon of Paris'; and then the tragedy of *Le Viol de Lucrèce* ('La grande Rome est en histoire'). No English group, in the same texts, has made any comparable effect. Norman Marshall, in *The Producer and the Play*[4], thought of Tarquin 'miming his way through the dark corridors of the sleeping palace, feeling his way with outstretched hands through the blackness, losing himself among the winding passages, hesitating, retracing his way, stumbling over unseen steps, fumbling with unfamiliar locks, until at last he forces the door of the bedchamber with his knee'. On the little stage of the Arts Theatre, Marshall said, 'the actor was never more than a few feet away from the bed as he mimed his journey through the palace, yet so completely had we been induced to forget the conventions of the realistic theatre that the bed, instead of being an incongruous distraction, became the symbol of Tarquin's desire; we saw it not as a tangible object but as the image burning in Tarquin's brain, drawing him irresistibly towards the crime'.

Nothing comparable occurred in 1932 though we can observe, among the chaos of titles, a piece named *As It Was in the Beginning,* first draft of what was to be an enormously popular sentimental comedy, *The Wind and the Rain,* by a young New Zealand-born doctor, Merton Hodge. Far more important—though an Arts play only by courtesy—a historical chromicle, *Richard of Bordeaux,* came from 'Gordon Daviot', one of the pseudonyms ('Josephine Tey' was another) of a Scottish writer, Elizabeth Mackintosh. Bronson Albery, considering at first that it took some courage to compete with Shakespeare, was unsure. His wife Una urged him to accept. At length he put £300 into two trial performances, 'presented by the Arts Theatre Club' on the stage of the New, obviously better fitted to complex scene changes. *Richard of Bordeaux*—which remains in spirit, at least, an Arts play—allowed John

Gielgud to translate into a sensitive prose idiom the lyric portrait of Richard II he had acted at the Old Vic in the autumn of 1929.

At that time the Arts system allowed both for Sunday-night plays and for runs of half-a-dozen performances, from Tuesday to the next Sunday (an occasion which, if Press criticism had been good—and in those days it counted a lot—would be the money-maker). Expenses, by modern standards, were nominal: thus John Fernald managed to do Emlyn Williams' early piece, *The Vigil,* for £80, and C.K. Munro's *Mr. Eno, His Birth, Death, and Life* for £120. Actors (we can imagine the horror of Equity in the 1980s) received £5; scenery, as a rule, was old material repainted. Performances could be first-rate; the Arts was recognised as a theatre in which to try your luck, and many major players did so.

Not that so applauded a company as the Pitoëffs' needed any special talisman when it crossed from Paris with several productions in February 1933. The centre was *La Ronde* when Mme. Pitoëff, an actress of sharp immediacy, appeared as the five women in Schnitzler's chain of brief scenes, an anecdote ten times repeated. During the following month an English cast under Tyrone Guthrie, not very well known then, bore off Dorothy Massingham and Murray Macdonald's tragedy, *The Lake,* which went to the Westminster with Marie Ney's transfiguring emotional clarity.

On Shakespeare's Birthday this year, Sir Philip Ben Greet staged, principally for collectors, the First Quarto text of *Hamlet.* He had done it at the Arts four years earlier, with John Wyse; now Donald Wolfit, once Claudius to Gielgud in the Folio version, drove vigorously at the part, wearing H.B. Irving's black tunic, lent to him by Tom Heslewood. Thea Holme was the girl here called Ofelia, and Greet himself the Corambis (Polonius).

Soon afterwards, and despite a membership of four thousand, the Arts found itself in deep trouble. On July 4, 1933, Mr. Justice Bennett ordered it to be compulsorily wound up; and on August 3, in Bankruptcy Buildings, Carey Street, the Official Receiver presided at the statutory meetings of creditors and shareholders under the winding-up order. The company, it was said, had been registered in December 1925 with a nominal capital of £100, increased to £250 in the next June. £18,567 went upon the erection of theatre and club premises (registered as the Arts Theatre Club), necessary finance provided by the issue of debentures and by an advance from the bankers, secured by charges on the lease of the premises and by guarantees.

During the past two years patronage had dwindled, and with it the number of plays. Accounts for the year ending on April 30, 1932, showed a loss of £2,273, with a further loss of £4,524 in the ensuing twelve months. Failure and insolvency were attributed to trade depression. The directors explained that, as a 'luxury' business, it had insufficient support from its members to be run at a profit. A statement of affairs revealed gross liabilities of £29,668 of which £17,499 was expected to rank, and assets of £3,094: with these absorbed, however, by debenture and preferential claims, there could be nothing for unsecured creditors. The meetings decided to leave the liquidation in the hands of the Official Receiver.

For another five months the theatre was dark. Then, on February 9, 1934, *The Times* reported that the Arts would re-open on February 28 under a new committee which had bought the assets of the old club; Basil Ionides, who had redecorated it, had also made some structural alterations. The policy would still be to present plays of artistic merit and of a kind unlikely to appear in the commercial theatre; moreover (an unrealised hope) films from time to time would represent various schools of production. Already more than 2,000 applications had come in for proposed 'founder membership' of 750; associates would pay a nominal subscription.

The actual re-opening date was March 4, 1934; the play, Ibsen's *A Doll's House* in the Archer text; Lydia Lopokova as a frail Nora escaping from the toils of Walter Hudd's Torvald. During May, Irene Hentschel, Ivor Brown's wife, who specialised then in the fragile inventions of Jean-Jacques Bernard, directed *The Springtime of Others;* and, close upon this, Tyrone Guthrie, fresh from his testing season at the Vic, staged Norman Ginsbury's expertly biographical *Viceroy Sarah* with Edith Evans as Sarah, Duchess of Marlborough. Three of James Bridie's friends, under the collective pseudonym of 'T.J. Mellish' (one of them was Dr. T.J. Honeyman) put up £150 for three performances of his *Colonel Wotherspoon,* and they made a minute profit.

Unfortunately, the management originated fewer and fewer productions, preferring to let the Arts to societies in need of a home. Things had begun to sag when Bronson Albery, having more valuable work to do in his own theatres, grew less active. Up at the Embassy in Swiss Cottage Ronald Adam seemed to be getting the best of the new scripts (apart from those in Norman Marshall's excitingly idiosyncratic regime at the Gate). Some of the Arts plays during its second period of decline were not a little eccentric, though it would be wrong to write off these years entirely. Yet, owned then by the deaf Harold Rubins, a former Australian sheep-farmer, who lived with his aspiring actress-wife in the upper flat, it was neither a prized shop-window nor the once fashionable rendezvous where Emlyn Williams,[5] looking in to read the papers, would spot those 'well-known players hurrying in and out between shows'. Norman Marshall, who was taking the Gate up while the Arts slipped quietly down, was not being cynical when he wrote in *The Other Theatre*[6] (1946): 'Looking through a typical year's work during the Thirties (1936) one finds an extraordinary hotch-potch of shows ranging from Hasenclever's *Ehen Werden in Himmel Geschlossen,* presented by J.T. Grein's Cosmopolitan Theatre, to *And So To Bed,* acted by a Jewish Girls' Club.'

Clearly, there was no kind of play-policy at the Arts, and with every season the regulars depressingly drained away. Nevertheless, loyalists could be gratified. In the spring of 1936 Rodney Ackland's best comedy, *After October,* went from the Arts to the Criterion. That season, too, Eric Portman had the right flamboyant attack as Byron in *Bitter Harvest* by Catherine Turney, among the more literate of the dramatic biographies popular during the Thirties. Esmond Knight appeared in 1937 as Van Gogh in a play of that name and of some character. Written by a former Irish jockey and horse-trainer, Dan McKenna, Knight[7] wrote of it in his autobiography, *Seeking the Bubble:* 'Perhaps too macabre to be a popular success, it deserved a better fate than four performances at the Arts Theatre Club.'

In the coming year Denis Johnston's subtle adaptation of the German dramatist Ernst Toller's *The Blind Goddess*—re-christened *Blind Man's Buff* and directed by Fernald—should have got a West End home without delay; it had to wait another fifteen years. The narrative might have dithered at the start and dallied towards the end, but between these points Toller and Johnston had composed a trial scene uncommonly tense and based upon the handling of an extract from the laws of evidence. (Justice, according to a bitter woman, was a game of blind man's buff.)

Forward, presently, to the deadening outbreak of war; one play aside, little happened at the Arts between 1939 and 1941 except a series of short ballet programmes ('Lunch, After Lunch, and Tea-Time Ballet') by the Rambert dancers. The production in September 1940—which might have been devised for the period—was *The Infernal Machine,* an over-heated restatement of the Oedipus theme and the inexorable working of destiny, by the Frenchman, Jean Cocteau. The tiny Threshold Theatre had been visualising a production that was much too big for the house; it was decided to do it at the Arts instead, but there, immediately on opening with a redoubtable cast (and costumes by Oliver Messel), the blitz on London began and the company had to keep to matinees.

For eighteen months the theatre was dark. It would be the spring of 1942 before the Arts Theatre Club, which many people in those bewildering years believed had vanished for ever, was suddenly and dramatically re-born.

1   *Manchester Guardian,* 6.1.1929.
2   Re-titled *She Passed Through Lorraine* on transfer.
3   *Sunday Times,* 12.6.1931; reprinted in *Red Letter Nights* (Cape, 1944, p. 16).
4   *The Producer and the Play* (Macdonald, 1957), pp. 64–5.
5   *Emlyn* (Bodley Head, 1973), p. 101: "Robert Douglas, Adrianne Allen, Maurice Evans, Ursula Jeans, Jack Hawkins, Ann Todd, Roger Livesey, Jane Baxter, Laurence Olivier, who looked—with a black Ronald-Colman moustache and a black Anthony-Eden Homburg—like a smouldering Under-Secretary. They all seemed sociable, with the easy movements of success."
6   *The Other Theatre* (Lehmann, 1947), p. 215.
7   Hutchinson (n.d.), p. 117.

CHAPTER TWO
ENTER CLUNES: 1942–1944

In a frigid spring, coldest for a long time, and with the country near the middle of a war that appeared to have begun in a legendary world, an actor just thirty years old entered the run-down theatre in Great Newport Street and, within a couple of months, had lifted its fortunes. Not strictly handsome but able to seem so, six feet two inches in height, with a great deal of charm (quite unsynthetic), a certain obstinate resolve, and a voice already potentially magnificent in its richness, his name was Alec Sheriff de Moro Clunes.

Born in Brixton, he was the son of an actor of Cornish birth and Scottish descent, who among much else had been Matheson Lang's expert stage manager. Alec went to school at Cliftonville, thence into advertising, and at length tried specialised journalism. He founded and partly edited a short-lived publication, *The Amateur Theatre and Playwrights' Journal.* Unlike many theorists, he sought to practise his own theories; through four years during the early 1930s he acted with and directed for societies—amateur but on the professional fringe—at Croydon and at the Tavistock Little Theatre in Bloomsbury. In the Croydon Histrionic Society he was glad to have the friendship, which developed into permanent advice, of an older amateur player, F.O.M. (Frank) Smith, whose knowledge of accountancy and the theatre would be invaluable one day to Alec and the Arts.

Obsessed by the stage, he thought of no other career. After brief interludes with Ben Greet's Pastoral Players, and repertory in Croydon and Seaford, he joined at 21, and in the autumn of 1933, the Old Vic company in Waterloo Road. There, after a number of minor character parts, among them Friar Francis (dressed self-consciously as a Greek Orthodox priest) in Henry Cass's capricious *Much Ado About Nothing,* and Gilles de Rais ('Bluebeard') in *Saint Joan,* he was a roaring, ginger-headed Pistol (*Henry IV, Part II*), muffled by a Falstaff who gained barely a single laugh. So, finally, to acting Laertes (to Maurice Evans) in *Hamlet,* the 'eternity' text as well as the usual compression. Any junior at the Vic had to work for his five pounds a week.

Clunes had a second Old Vic season (1935–36) after being replaced, as the young dope addict, in the London company of Merton Hodge's *Grief Goes Over* when the piece ended its provincial tour. A rap for any player; a bigger one for Clunes who had given himself without stint to his study of technique, and who would not realise until Sybil Thorndike soothed him, that somebody with a 'West End name' was needed. He felt it so much that, thereafter, when a manager himself and sometimes reputed to be ruthless, he did his best not to hurt anyone by a comparable dismissal. (If he did not always succeed, he did try.) During his second Old Vic season he could listen, night by night, to Ion Swinley, among the great might-have-beens of the English stage, and he learnt much from Swinley's control of an extraordinary voice. Clunes was acting more fluently now; Tyrone Guthrie, a mesmeric director, who succeeded Henry Cass in the autumn of 1936, spotted the young man's quality and cast him for a zestful Berowne in *Love's Labour's Lost* and for a first professional periwig-part (Harcourt) in *The Country Wife*.

Briskly, during the next five years, he was all over the place. His worst luck was in *The Road to Ruin* at the Ambassadors; Hay Petrie, as the rattling Goldfinch, developed complete amnesia and surrendered to the first-night prompter; ensuing notices wrecked the production. Clunes had better fortune: a return to the Vic, as Clarence and Tyrrel to the Richard III, synthesis of cat and goblin, of Emlyn Williams; the creation of the barnstorming Mr. Bassett Laneworthy-Figg, 'late of many Theatres Royal and now our own Resident Tragedian', at the Players' Theatre Club; and seasons at Malvern (1938) and, as Coriolanus, Benedick and Iago, at Stratford-upon-Avon (1939, the theatre's diamond jubilee). War cut this short; Clunes went to a hastily assembled repertory cast at Oxford, returning to London (1940) as the reprehensible Horner of *The Country Wife* at the Little (soon to be shattered by bombing), and as Godfrey Kneller in Shaw's autumnal idea of the Restoration, *In Good King Charles's Golden Days,* at the New. (Shaw would always be his preferred modern dramatist.)

By then, after seven years as a professional, he had established himself as a principal actor of the new generation. Guthrie, responsible for the Old Vic companies centred for a while on the Lancashire town of Burnley, sent him on tour, as Malvolio and as Young Marlow (*She Stoops To Conquer*). Good; but by no means enough for Alec Clunes who had the boldest idea of what he wished to see in a theatre, and how, granted the chance, he could run that theatre himself. Within a year he had passed from actor to actor-manager in one of the most potentially important, certainly least prophesied, stage moves of its day: the rescue of the languishing Arts.

During that late spring and early summer of 1942 the Arts Theatre Club was in virtual collapse. Yet Clunes, who seldom hesitated when he had made up his mind—he was buttressed by the sagacity of Frank

Smith who had watched him through the years—spied here the platform he wanted. The London theatre (the Vic had been bombed) was in a dreary state; it could do with such a club as the Arts that might serve also as the major Repertory the West End lacked. In a swiftly-compiled prospectus Clunes wrote: 'We believe that there is an audience in London eager for intelligent and entertaining plays; for a theatre whose policy, without being highbrow, is yet opposed to the monotony of the leg-show and the dullness of the average West End drawing-room piece. We believe that this audience can best be served by a consistent policy of plays and personnel established at one central theatre premises. We believe that the Arts Theatre Club (just by Leicester Square Tube Station), under our management as from 20 April 1942, is ideally suited to our purpose. The amenities of the Club include an intimate Theatre, well equipped, pleasant to look at, and comfortable to sit in; a large and comfortable *Restaurant,* a large, sunny, comfortably furnished Lounge, Bar, Theatre Snack Bar, and accommodation for dancing and club functions.'

It sounded all right, yet many considered Clunes to be headstrong, even a trifle mad, to take over a small club theatre with a handful of members (only 200) at a moment when audiences were easily put off by air-raids, actors were scarce, and scenery hard to get. Still (at the moment anyway), he had the goodwill of James Agate of the *Sunday Times,* probably the most influential contemporary critic. Clunes, as a classical and romantic actor, had been on one of Agate's short lists; on an American visit in 1937 he confided to his journal[1] (among those public confidences): 'There is nobody over here with the quality of Charles Laughton, John Gielgud, Laurence Olivier, Ralph Richardson, Stephen Haggard, Robert Eddison, Alec Clunes, to mention only a few.' So when Clunes told him five years later of the plan to restore the Arts, Agate not only cheered in private; he did so in print. Writing in the *Sunday Times* on April 19, 1942, he agreed with everything in the Arts credo. He was glad, in particular, that the venture would not be run for a profit, 'meaning that whatever profits accrue will be put into further plays'; that prices would be reasonable; that the star system would not prevail; and that, though there was a certain amount of capital behind the venture, it was not enough to take responsibility from the public— assuming that the new theatre did, in fact, present plays that were 'intelligent and *entertaining*' (Agate's italics).

There had, in the event, to be changes in the tentative programme Clunes had suggested to Agate. This was Sean O'Casey's *Purple Dust* (which its Second Workman called 'a gold embroidery of dancin' words'); Shakespeare's *Twelfth Night;* Clifford Odets' American piece of lower-middle-class realism, *Awake and Sing;* and Clifford Bax's

Socrates, an act of healing in Periclean Athens. For *Purple Dust,* which O'Casey refused to release, Clunes substituted *The Sulky Fire* by Jean-Jacques Bernard; *Socrates* was shelved; and finally the opening plays were settled as *Awake and Sing, Twelfth Night* (Clunes would never have omitted this), a double bill of *The Springtime of Others* and Chekhov's *Swan Song,* and G.K. Chesterton's *Magic* preceded by another short Chekhov, *The Proposal.* No Shaw.

Clunes had needed a capital of £1,500. By finding this sum his American friend, Beecher Moore, enabled the enterprise to begin. Members (and 6,000 were required, the former Arts list thirty times multiplied), began to arrive at the rate of 100 a day, encouraged by the prospectus and a good deal of heartening publicity. Full members in 1942 paid two guineas a year, with access to club amenities and the right to reserve tickets for themselves and their friends; theatre members paid a five-shilling annual subscription (with admission to the snack bar). Ticket prices were as reasonable as they could be: 7s.6d (37½p), 5s. (25p), and 3s.6d. (17½p), tax included.

Clunes announced that, besides Shakespeare, he intended to present the Restoration comedies and, especially, Farquhar's neglected *The Constant Couple* (clearly Sir Harry Wildair had been on his mind); a fresh translation of Molière's *Tartuffe;* and really good new plays that had not appealed to any commercial management. 'In short we shall attempt to bring together good plays and good actors, present them to the best of our ability, and hope to interest in them a selective but not exclusive audience. It is our hope and belief that from this will grow spontaneously a policy that will have both success and integrity.' Clunes had written better than this, but behind the flat phrasing was a resolute belief.

The new Arts, leased from the Cranbourn Estate at £14 a week for the entire building, opened on May 20, 1942; its curtain rose that night as early as six o'clock, essential under the pall of the war-time black-out. The play was Odets' picture of the lower middle class in the Bronx, *Awake and Sing;* Clunes, who had had faith in it since two Stage Society performances in 1938, directed himself, with a cast which, since it was a historical Arts occasion, we give in full:

Myron Berger	John Ruddock
Ralph Berger	Richard Attenborough
Hennie Berger	Vivienne Bennett
Jacob	Martin Miller
Bessie	Lilly Kann
Moe Axelrod	Julian Somers
Uncle Morty	Harry Ross

| Sam Feinschriber | Denys Blakelock |
| Schlosser | Fred Berger |

Helped by its admirable reviews, the production caused unusual excitement in a West End that needed it; Richard Attenborough, 18-year-old son of the Principal of University College, Leicester, rose to his first real chance. Remarkably, considering pre-war runs at the Arts, the play lasted for nearly three weeks, and in August had another three on the big stage of the Cambridge Theatre in Seven Dials. Not much for the records, maybe, but it had made West End audiences aware of the changes in Great Newport Street. A critic who described *Awake and Sing* as a title of good omen had the right feeling.

Twelfth Night followed. Wisely, and typically, Clunes had not taken the slightest notice of Agate's capricious warning not to do Shakespeare in general, and *Twelfth Night* in particular. The comedy meant a lot to him. He had acted Aguecheek at Stratford (1939) where Lionel Hale, of the *News Chronicle,* had described him cheerfully as 'like a wild picture of the youngest, ugliest, and most unpopular member of a Victorian bicycling club'; and he had also toured as Malvolio for the Vic. This time he decided to direct it himself and to act Feste, and he changed the opening so that, instead of going immediately to Orsino's court and 'If music be the food of love, play on', the action began upon the Illyrian shore where Jean Forbes-Robertson's grave child of a Viola had been wrecked. Walter Hudd was a relentlessly gouty Malvolio; Denys Blakelock approached Aguecheek as a case of arrested development (Ernest Milton's suggestion); Vivienne Bennett, whose Arts work was some of her happiest, played Olivia; Joyce Redman (not yet a star) Maria, and Russell Thorndike a Toby alarmingly bibulous. Richard Attenborough had little to do this time except to be Jean Forbes-Robertson's twin, which might have been considered work enough for one evening. On the whole the night satisfied Clunes and—more to the point just then—the critics.

The always difficult double bills followed, Chekhov–Bernard and Chesterton–Chekhov. *Magic,* long unseen in London, depended mainly upon Stanford Holme as its inconsequential Chestertonian Duke who is reminded, in the most inexplicable fashion, of such irrelevances as the French Revolution, the Spanish Inquisition, and Mr. Gladstone. Clunes played the posing magician. Capital fun, it caused no special stir. Excitement was offstage one evening; the discovery that burglars had stolen essential clothes—tails and white ties—worn by members of the cast. There was nothing to do but cancel the performance though, fortunately, this would not be a regular event.

The relaxed atmosphere of the new Arts was what people needed in the depth of the war (a good many refugees had joined, and they stayed faithful, whatever the company put on). By October 1942 a splendid potential audience was ready for a new 'tragi-comedy', *House of Regrets.* Clunes had made it known that he would welcome valuable new work; and here, on its cue, he staged a piece by a young actor-dramatist, Peter Ustinov, with a cosmopolitan background. Remembered from the Players', he had satirised there an Austro-German operatic diva and lieder singer named, improbably, Mme. Liselotte Beethoven-Finck. (He, or she, was now to be under the management of Bassett Laneworthy-Figg.) His play, highly atmospheric, about a party of White Russians dreaming in a Baron's Court boarding-house of a Czarist revolution, had been written in school exercise-books when he was nineteen and waiting in his Wyndham's dressing-room during the Farjeon revue, *Diversion.*[2] Now the young man was gratified by a press that he said later he had never had before and never known since.[3]

It was this that sealed the reputation of the Arts Group of Actors. Clunes knew that he could carry on safely; in spite of the 'Group' label, the Arts was one man's adventure, backed by the wisdom of his advisers. He pleased everyone next with a revival of *Maria Marten,* written ostensibly by 'the Hon——— (a Gentleman)' which could quite easily have been bred at the Players' and had indeed its favourite Joanna Horder to sing 'Kind Heaven, Content, and a Cot'. Clunes enjoyed directing this so much that he chose a second, and similar, extravaganza for Christmas. Before this, though, he did another new play, the first at the Arts by James Bridie since that nearly forgotten *Colonel Wotherspoon.* Called *Holy Isle,* and set in the never-never Orkneys of 1,500 years before, it had an agreeably impudent sub-title, 'The impact of civilisation on the age of innocence, or some such tilly-vally'. As a tilly-vally it could be engaging—with such characters as Ku, She, Qua, Kwoo, and Sir Lachlan of the Cats—but on the whole text transcended performance. The Christmas successor to *Maria Marten* was the 'celebrated temperance tract', *The Drunkard,* by W.H. Smith and a Gentleman. Written many years earlier for P.T. Barnum, it ended, when the dying hero had been persuaded to sign the pledge, with an optimistic line, 'There is hope for the Drunkard, thank God'. Harold Scott directed with his straight-faced zest, and the Arts moved into 1943, its membership flourishing and with an optimism of its own.

The theatre's nightly opening had been put forward to 6.30 (in the summer months it would be seven o'clock). New members realised that the promise of true repertory had not been a mirage. During the first half of the year dramatists included Shaw (*Androcles and the Lion*) and Goldsmith, Synge (*The Well of the Saints*), and Paul Vincent Carroll (*The Old Foolishness*). Clunes, if then lacking a little in dynamism (something no one would say again of this particular performance) had an eloquent evening with *Don Juan in Hell:* Shaw on most matters between music, 'the brandy of the damned', and creative evolution. But the joy of 1943—midway the theatre had reached 10,000 members—was a Festival of English Comedy, recalled now for Farquhar's *The Constant Couple* and Pinero's *The Magistrate.* Dressed elaborately and without the use of a single clothing coupon, *The Constant Couple* (sets and costumes by Rolf Gerard and Fanny Taylor) now returned to London after a century-and-a-half: usually an agreeable rattle, brisk and graceless, all the one-way traffic of Park, Mall, and piazza, not to speak of the neighbouring 'rummers' and the hold of Newgate. Sir Harry Wildair, 'affecting humorous gaiety and freedom in his behaviour', is grand company, a Restoration Berowne whom Clunes turned into a flashing kingfisher of comedy. Though cast in strength—particularly David Bird as the Alderman who becomes a kind of period Widow Twankey, and Robert Marsden, all black-browed night as Vizard ('outwardly pious, otherwise a great Debauchee and villainous') everything rested on Clunes' disciplined vigour, his disarming smile, and his good-tempered impatience when the amiable libertine mistakes for a bawdy-house the home of Angelica: we have not forgotten his Burgundy-exhilarated entrance, his disbelieving 'Woof!' ('a noise', said someone, 'like an amiable Labrador'), or the cry, 'Wit and manners! Egad now I conceive there is a great deal of wit and manners in twenty guineas'.

This was a superb creation; incidentally, the last part that Clunes—who himself directed—played at the Arts for more than a year. His engagement in heavy rescue work at St. Pancras occupied a lot of his time: a routine of 24 hours on, 24 hours off, made life difficult. Yet with his commitments he contrived to read every night, in his flat above the theatre, one of a heap of new scripts. The Arts had announced its first play competition, suggested by William Wordsworth who was one of the pillars of the theatre. A direct descendant of the poet and known affectionately as 'Uncle Bill', he was a splendid publicist who found himself diverted into many tasks besides publicity. Clunes was by no means eager to see people, even distinguished guests, and Wordsworth would do this tactfully. He had, too, such unexpected chores as 'papering' the house for dress rehearsals (technical rehearsals now), something that could be a problem. Probably because he wanted to avoid a war-time atmosphere, Clunes was dubious about too many uniforms in the audience.

The ten weeks' Festival of Comedy took place in the late summer of 1943, all the plays dressed in costumes that had been designed for a Ben Greet American tour; there were over two hundred of these, in thirty hampers, that could be altered in the theatre or entirely re-made.

The Rivals, following the Farquhar, had Denys Blakelock as an endearing Acres who never for a moment confused 'Fighting Bob' with Tony Lumpkin; in fact he appeared more at home on the North Parade than he would have been at Clod Hall. Blakelock had always thought it wrong to see him as a bucolic; rather he could be a kind of second cousin to Sir Andrew Aguecheek. Soon the same actor enjoyed a strenuous night out as Aeneas Posket (of Mulberry Street) in *The Magistrate.* Popular during the 1880s, Pinero's farces had been overwhelmed by his serious plays (though *The Magistrate* did service in 1917 as a musical-comedy libretto, *The Boy,* for W.H. Berry). It was left to the Arts to return it to its proper function. Among the most meticulous actors of his time—his autobiography, *Finding My Way,* reinforces this—Blakelock's care for technique delighted another obsessed technician, Alec Clunes, who wrote to him reminiscently: 'One of my best-remembered joys was waiting each morning to see what you had thought up (or refined) during your painstaking hours of homework.'

Besides Blakelock, setting his house in order with a breathless benignity, and wearing the abundant 'Dundrearies' he remembered from the lawyer Sir Edward Clarke, the company included Avice Landone as the triumphant Mrs. Posket; David Bird and Bill Shine. It was sad that, more than a year later, when the play with its Arts cast in full surge had the chance of a West End run at the St. Martin's, it had soon to come off, a victim of the onrush of flying bombs which affected London audiences.

As for *Misalliance,* another of the Festival of comedies (during the Clunes era one-seventh of his choices were Shavian), John Tarleton's house-party, augmented by a clutch of aviators in the Hindhead summer of 1910, talked on without an interval for two hours and twenty minutes. Secondary Shaw maybe, but sport royal, especially when Peter Jones as the Cockney clerk, poor shot but good Marx man, uttered his devastating prophecy: 'Rome fell; Babylon fell; Hindhead's turn will come.' GBS, invariably a friend to the Arts—though he did disappoint Clunes by withholding permission for a full *Man and Superman*—arrived at a Sunday matinee. William Wordsworth entertained him in the office where he was extremely genial ('You like my plays here, don't you?') but refused tea and sandwiches, saying that he must get back to Whitehall Court: Wordsworth watched him striding off, with knickerbockers and stick, down St. Martin's Lane. He was then 87; his membership card was presented to the theatre committee after his death in 1950. Later plays in 1943 would be less exhilarating, though this made no difference whatever to a progressively mounting membership which could hardly have counted on Shaw every month.

1   *Ego 3* (Harrap, 1938), p. 157
2   *Dear Me* (Heinemann, 1977), p. 104.
3   Ibid., p. 118.

CHAPTER THREE
HIGH NOON: 1944–1948

With so small an auditorium, very few plays would make money. Hence the needed minimum of 6,000 members which had appeared so distant during the tentative months of 1942, but which by 1944 had been an accomplished fact for some time. That spring Clunes directed Peter Powell's prizewinning comedy, *The Two Children,* chosen from nearly six hundred scripts; the winner was a naval lieutenant who had heard of the competition while in the wardroom of *King George V* in Mediterranean waters. Clunes said he had read no new play with so much admiration since Ustinov's *House of Regrets.* A good-natured study of manners, it became less satisfying towards the end when the people lost their clear outline and the narrative did fade inconclusively. Still, it acted agreeably throughout; Jean Cadell's matriarchal Lady Harriet governed the night, a personage, said the *Punch* critic, who sat with dignity in the saddle, 'o'erlooking all the war'.

The year's other productions were as various as ever; audiences did not droop. *The Witch,* based by John Masefield on a Norwegian original, proved to be a sombre evening, exciting at times. Richard Wordsworth, as a young man troubled by an amorous stepmother, presently moved with ease to the testing title-part of Shaw's second comedy, *The Philanderer,* looking—tawny-bearded and knickerbockered—remarkably like the young GBS. Jean-Jacques Bernard's *The Sulky Fire* was a post-Armistice anecdote, strangely drab and irresolute, but its author had been in favour for some time and he would remain so.

Bird in Hand reminded us that John Drinkwater, dramatist of *Abraham Lincoln,* was not altogether wedded to the graver historical chronicles. With Herbert Lomas as its heart of oak, a yeoman innkeeper from the Cotswolds, the piece caused at least one playgoer to laugh so much that he telephoned to offer £2,000 towards a West End run; sadly, on transference to the St. Martin's it had no special luck. Clunes, who directed (at the moment he preferred direction to acting) also put on Goldoni's *Mine Hostess* in the Bax version, Baliol Holloway as the haughty misogynist overthrown by the mistress of the house. Near the end of the run, where he had been richly in period, 'Bay' had to leave for a peculiarly stupid West End musical which sank without trace; at the Arts Clunes took over the Knight of Ripafratta during the last few performances. This was the year, too, of Denys Blakelock in Maugham's *The Breadwinner* which James Agate, who could be something of a trial in those days, endangered by facetiously (and inaccurately) headlining his *Sunday Times* notice, 'Mr. Blakelock Ruins a Play'; Dorothy Reynolds as O'Neill's Anna Christie, involved with a tempestuous Irish stoker; and at Christmas, Hugh Burden—who, among other more obvious recommendations, was a cousin of Mrs. Patrick Campbell—as Mr. Puff, 'practitioner in panegyric', in Sheridan's marvellous parody, *The Critic,* which had been badly neglected; soon its time would come again with a production by the Old Vic company where it partnered, of all plays, *Oedipus.* At the Arts now, an inventive revival, in which Judith Furse dutifully piled galleon upon fire-ship, had its unexpected offstage problems: the load of work just then had become overwhelming, and when the wardrobe mistress did not turn up one night before Christmas, Clunes invited actresses to stay behind and get on with the sewing. Until daybreak he entertained them with coffee and recitation.

Keeping up its Shavian run, the Arts early in 1945 staged a rarity, *The Simpleton of the Unexpected Isles.* Shaw was the only living dramatist who, if he wished, could produce the Day of Judgment and unleash its apocalyptic thunders. But audiences were uncertain what he was driving at in a fable now of polygamy in the Pacific, now of a herald angel, tetchily genial, who wings from the empyrean to sound the Last Trump. So far as they could gather, he was comparing human values: Judgment Day was one of valuation, and those found wanting would vanish into air. But the sage remained inexplicit. Audiences panted after him expectantly. Judith Furse directed the allegory-cum-intellectual farce without fighting for effect, and Peter Jones was sweetly the Simpleton (his ultimate 'silliness' in the Elizabethan sense), a young clergyman called Phosphor Hammingtap: Shaw could never be trusted with a christening.

By now, with thirteen thousand members, the new Arts had settled so firmly into the London theatre scene that it seemed preposterous even to hint that, only three years before, it had been abandoned in the desert. Indeed, during the summer of 1945, Clunes and his fellow-directors were able to buy the lease for £20,000. The restaurant, under the guidance of Haridemos Johannides ('Jo'), was again the artistic rendezvous it had been during the primeval period of the late 1920s, and Clunes could be seen there on most days at his table discreetly placed.

Undoubtedly, the Arts never lacked advertisement. James Agate, unpredictable pontiff of the *Sunday Times,* who had believed that he ought to be a kind of father confessor to the theatre, felt that he was being under-employed. Certainly Clunes was not consulting him. Though he had advised against Shaw (as well as *Twelfth Night*) most critics agreed with the Arts policy, and Agate was banging his head against the wall, an exercise he seldom enjoyed. Now he went off on another course. In his weekly article of August 13, 1944, he began by deciding to his own satisfaction that the Arts was interested in all centuries but this and every country but its own. After the opening shot he declared that he had discovered a splendid play about shirkers in war-time, a piece with a single set and a cast of ten, 'a little miracle of craftsmanship', based on the theme of the Prime Minister's 'Come then; let us to the task, to the battle, to the times, each to our part, each to our station'. The play, by a veteran dramatist, H.F. Maltby (1880–1963), and called *The Compleat Wangler* (later wisely re-named *The Wanglers*) was about people who left the task and the battle to others and who got themselves safe jobs at home. 'An admirable corrective,' Agate continued, 'to the sentimentalities of the Mrs. Miniver order,' it was an astringent experience, and he would lay 100 to 1 that the Arts would not do it.

He had no idea what he had taken on. In the next issue of *The Sunday Times* Clunes wrote an open letter which began: 'You concluded by most rashly laying 100 to 1 against our presenting the play. Subject to certain conditions indicated below, I here and now accept this offer and enclose £10 herewith—I shall expect my £1,000 on the first night.' He went on to say that a play on shirkers in war-time was not a fair picture of what war was about. It was his most serious belief that *The Compleat Wangler* offered a 'hideously distorted, graceless and ungrateful view of those "who also serve" and who have suffered so much so bravely'.

For all that, despite personal dislike of the piece and knowledge that West End managers had rejected it, Clunes was prepared to present it at the Arts on his own conditions: that the run was limited to two 'try-out' weeks, the actors to receive their usual salaries (all other expenses on the usual Arts standard); that Agate should direct and assemble the cast at the regular fee of £50; and that after the production, he, Clunes, should have Agate's space in *The Sunday Times*. Agate, responding, declined the offer to direct ('Maltby himself should do it and should also be cast as Chief Wangler'): 'What I will do to help is to sit in during rehearsals to make sure that sentimentality has been kept at arm's length and that the play's satire is allowed to stand forth in all its naked savagery.'

That was that. Nothing more happened, of course: *The Compleat Wangler*, naked savagery or not, was never staged in the West End[1] and the Arts—doubtless to Agate's irritation—went forward to Shaw: a production of *Fanny's First Play* without (as so often) its prologue and epilogue, and, early in 1945, *The Simpleton*. These were succeeded by *An Italian Straw Hat* (Labiche and Marc-Michel), *The Government Inspector* (Gogol), *A Doll's House* (Ibsen), and the romantic anecdote (James Laver from Klabund) of *The Circle of Chalk,* all matters upon which Agate was silent. Christopher Fry, former young schoolmaster and actor and a coming major dramatist, directed *The Circle of Chalk* and inserted its best line, 'I am like a cushion upon which Life has lately been sitting'. Pamela Brown had introduced him to Judith Furse; in turn she recommended him to Clunes. Hence his direction of the Chinese play, and later of *The School for Scandal.*

It was also about now, in mid-1945, that a young man named Peter Brook came into the Arts, engaging, assured, and with a cosmopolitan background. Aged twenty, he was seeking a job as a director. Since he left Oxford he had staged Cocteau's *The Infernal Machine* at the tiny Chanticleer, a theatre club in a crevice of South Kensington where Greta Douglas had a semi-permanent company; he had also revived *The Barretts of Wimpole Street* for Jack de Leon in the uncompromising barn of the Q at Kew Bridge. So far he was not particularly satisfied: 'I want to change and develop,' he wrote,[2] 'and dread the thought of standing still.' In this determined mood he reached Great Newport Street; Alec Clunes (whom twelve years later he would direct as Caliban in *The Tempest*) did not want to see him, so sent him along to talk to William Wordsworth. Among the plays the Arts wished to do sometime was a version of Jean-Paul Sartre's *Huis Clos,* under the title of *Vicious Circle,* and Brook confided to Wordsworth that this was a challenge he would love to meet.

'Uncle Bill' suggested that as the young man, among other languages, spoke excellent French, he should get in touch with Sartre and ask the dramatist himself to recommend him. This was another kind of challenge that delighted Brook; he duly went to Paris and hung about a writers' cafe on the Left Bank until, after a couple of nights, Sartre arrived; they talked; Sartre wrote the letter; and, in the summer of 1946, Brook, who had done a good deal meantime at the Birmingham Repertory and Stratford-upon-Avon, would duly direct *Huis Clos* at the Arts.

While Brook negotiated his future, the Arts was getting on with the second of its festivals, not this time confined to comedy. Christopher Fry directed *The School for Scandal;* Clunes, as he had long wished, acted Hamlet—he had a preliminary showing at the Arts in Cambridge, under Judith Furse—and other plays were Shaw's *Getting Married,* Pinero's *The Thunderbolt,* hardly a name to an Arts audience, and a revival of *The Constant Couple* which Clunes, by no means always eager to act, was anxious to do again for the sake of Sir Harry Wildair. After a variable provincial tour everything ended happily in London. If *Getting Married* was Shaw at his least theatrical, the Arts cast debated it loyally, though Olga Lindo clearly thought the ecstatic Mayoress a little troublesome, an awkward personage to be launched at our heads in a last act. Listeners, Shaw-trained, did not grumble; even so, Pinero's drama which, curiously, had failed at its première in 1908, was the more exciting night. The dramatist had a story to tell—where there's a will there's a way—and he kept closely to the point. An exact technician, Pinero had written many of his scenes, according to the usage of their time, as contemporary star-talk; but the Arts revival (with such people as Dorothy Reynolds, Mark Dignam, Roy Malcolm, Julian D'Albie and Margaret Vines) proved, under Peter Streuli's guidance, to be a team-play. As for a pocket edition of *The School for Scandal,* Fry's production was marked by the easy grace of Alec Clunes as Charles, often a man-trap if the actor is given to over-statement and a fussy period parade.

The Constant Couple (inevitably Clunes–Wildair) returned as the theatre's prized restoration. Finally, using the prerogative of an actor-manager, Clunes appeared as Hamlet (he was thirty-three). A portrait fruitful in pathos, it gained from the peculiar intimacy possible in so small a house where Hamlet could think aloud without straining, and it was a 'sweet prince' that the four captains bore like a soldier to the stage. Good; but this Hamlet did want the larger excitement; we waited for the great speeches to flower in fire. Throughout, Clunes expressed the prose more eloquently, on the whole, than the verse; his meditation among the tombs, with the tenderness of the apostrophe to Yorick, was exquisite in its reflective autumnal quality. It would be, in any event, the crown of the Festival, and Agate, continuing his idiosyncratic game of blowing hot and cold, praised the performance in a *Sunday Times* notice that said:[3] 'Let it be established, without further ado, that Mr. Clunes' Hamlet is a complete thing. Not the whole of Hamlet, perhaps, but complete as far as it goes.' Again: 'The point about this Hamlet is its extraordinarily human quality... Never in my life have I heard the *prose* in this great poem better spoken.'

While there had been a nightly programme-change in the first Arts Festival (of Comedy), every play in the second Festival was acted for a week at a time. That ought to have been easier, yet troubles did persist. With practically no wing-space, the storage of five elaborate productions simultaneously became a backstage headache. Various large pieces of furniture had to be strung up in the flies like so many hams. Though the Festival continued into the spring of 1946—in all, for over six months—it was clear that there could not be so adventurous a season again; even with consistently large houses there had to be a financial loss.

The Arts programme was usually surprising. When Ivor Brown, anxious to be complimentary, wrote in *The Observer* of 'a pocket National Theatre', Clunes corrected this immediately to 'International Theatre'. The year 1946 confirmed the label, with plays by Ibsen (*The Lady From the Sea*), Helge Krog (an oddly dispiriting Norwegian), August Defresne and Herman Heijermans (that Dutch interior, with Scandinavian influences, of *The Rising Sun*). Foreign guests apart, the late spring of 1946 is recalled for a loosely-contrived composite piece entitled *Exercise Bowler,* directed by Peter Powell (author of *The Two Children*), who, when demobilised from the Navy, reverted to direction, his principal love. The play had been inspired by the visit to the Arts in 1945 of the ABCA (Army Bureau of Current Affairs) Play Unit with two short documentaries. Clunes now invited the aid of Reunion Theatre, formed for demobilised actors and actresses, in staging a full-scale documentary about the return of a group of soldiers to civilian life. Five authors, writing as 'T. Atkinson', collaborated: Powell and Clunes, with Torin Thatcher and William Fox (both in the cast), and W.P. Templeton, the Arts' new 'dramatist-in-residence'. The result was satisfying, though everyone—the dramatists not least—was bewildered when a critic described the piece, portentously, as 'post-Pirandellian'.

The Arts had never ventured into Grand Guignol, but compared with that summer's production of *Huis Clos* (*Vicious Circle*), by the French existentialist, Jean-Paul Sartre, the Guignol paled its ineffectual fires. Today unexceptionable, it had still in 1946 to be acted technically in private. Peter Brook directed a version by Marjorie Gabain and Joan Swinstead. No longer a young man knocking at the gate, he had conquered with his Stratford *Love's Labour's Lost* and gone on to *The Brothers Karamazov* at Hammersmith; and Sartre's play might have been devised for his protean command of atmospherics. Its small room (designed here by Rolf Gerard), windowless, tarnished, airless, and furnished bleakly with three Second Empire sofas, red, electric-blue and spinach-green, was occupied by three people, a sadistic coward (Alec Guinness), a lesbian (Beatrix Lehmann), and a nymphomaniac (Betty Ann Davies). With the door shut, Hell had closed round them, a word that to Sartre meant a vast honeycomb where the condemned tortured each other by mere proximity. There the three victims of *Huis Clos* would exist forever, any two of them conscious of the deadly presence of the third; Brook directed with an ominous stillness, keeping the light fiercely unvaried in what the critic Siriol Hugh-Jones called 'a stuffy *cabinet particulier*'.[4] For years there had been nothing comparably terrifying on the London stage.

It was leagues from the political extravaganza of *The Apple Cart,* a Shavian debate with one of the longest parts (King Magnus) in modern

Plate 1. Exterior of the Arts Theatre Club, Great Newport Street, photographed in May 1952 (the poster is of *The Voysey Inheritance*). The building was designed by P. Morley Horder.
(*Photograph: K. Hutton; B.B.C. Hulton Picture Library*)

Plate 2. The première of Poet Laureate Robert Bridges' "comedy in the Spanish manner", *The Humours of the Court*, with Edith Evans at the Countess of Belflors. The Arts production in Janary 1930 came 37 years after completion of the play.

Plate 3. Leueen Macgrath as The Sphinx in Cocteau's *Infernal Machine*, produced at the Arts in September 1940.

drama. Clunes, dedicated Shavian, believed reasonably that Magnus would suit Jack Hawkins on leaving the Army for the theatre. Hawkins, who agreed with enthusiasm, wrote in his autobiography,[5] posthumously-published: 'Most of my friends thought I was quite mad to take on such a part for my return to the stage, but I thought I might as well have a go... It was one of the best decisions of my career.' He directed, with Peter Streuli; and Emma Trechman, as the King's mistress Orinthia, joined him in the catch-as-catch-can interlude.

A rare revival of Sheridan's *St. Patrick's Day; or, The Scheming Lieutenant*—its wit small beer rather than Madeira—occupied barely 55 minutes: such short commons that on the first night several people remained in their seats, unwilling to believe that the affair had ended. At any rate, it was pious of the Arts to do it and to complete nearly all of Sheridan. The last of the year's rediscoveries, George Lillo's *Fatal Curiosity* (1730) did take about an hour-and-a-half, but it is perilous to suppose that an ancient melodrama must necessarily be great fun when guyed for a modern audience. Luckily, by good plain speaking—and plain speech was the sovereign need—Hugh Griffith, as the father, suggested what *Fatal Curiosity* might be worth. Immediately before this revival (and later acted with it) Clunes chose Christopher Fry's enchantingly frivolous epistle from the Ephesians, *A Phoenix Too Frequent*, that had been performed at the Mercury earlier in 1946. Now it introduced to the Arts a young actor, Paul Scofield, who had been so touchingly dignified as Armado in Brook's Stratford *Love's Labour's Lost*. In the *Phoenix*, as the NCO who lost a body but found a wife (Hermione Hannen as Dynamene, widow of a coming man untimely gone), he swiftly destroyed any barrier between stage and audience. Exploiting the humours of incongruity, its comic pathos 'following the flickers of poetry', there had not been so engaging a short play for many years; in retrospect it rules the Arts story of 1946.

In 1947 the Arts divided its forces, sending a company abroad ('the English Arts Theatre'), sponsored by the British Council, directed by Peter Powell, and led by Fay Compton, Clunes, and Jack Hawkins. Forty people in all, with 25 tons of scenery and baggage, toured for 6,000 miles in seven countries: Czechoslovakia, Austria, Belgium, Holland, France, Italy and Switzerland. Useless as it is now to reduce this enterprise to a catalogue and gazetteer, there were four plays (*Don Juan in Hell, Hamlet, Othello* and *Candida*), and the mere list of places is daunting: Prague, Graz, Klagenfurt, Brussels, Liege, Ghent, Antwerp, The Hague, Amsterdam, Eindhoven, Utrecht, Rotterdam, Strasbourg, Cannes, Nice, Rome, Trieste, Milan, Florence and Zurich.

The influential firm of H.M. Tennent wanted to stage *Othello* at the Piccadilly Theatre when the company returned from Europe; but

Clunes—the Iago to Hawkins' Othello—had remained abroad on holiday, in Taormina, Sicily. It was difficult to get through to him. When at length he was located, he would not come back, refusing to believe it was a firm offer, though the Arts assured him that it was. Obstinately, when Tennents spoke to him, he still refused, so they gave it up and Anthony Quayle appeared as Iago in the West End run.

While the tour was on, the Arts company at home had worked upon the Shavian *Ring,* the complete sequence of that vast and intimidating work, *Back to Methuselah,* from primal innocence to the farthest reach of thought and the last utterance of Lilith, 'It is enough that there is a beyond'. Noel Willman, who directed, divided the plays into four instalments—Parts Two (*The Gospel of the Brothers Barnabas*) and Three (*The Thing Happens*) acted on the same night—and a new cyclorama made the stage look twice its size, a great help to the landscape of *In the Beginning.* There the testament of faith opens, as it ends, in a testament of beauty, with Genesis from that other pentateuch, and with the serpentine temptress ('I have willed and willed and willed') who indoctrinates Eve beneath the tree in Eden; as Vivienne Bennett played her, she spoke 'soft and almost silvery', and the night set audiences in good heart for the Shavian journey. Recalling that occasion in the early spring of 1947, W.A. Darlington (of the *Daily Telegraph*) wrote in his later autobiography[6]: 'For six excruciating weeks the drama critics of London had gone about their duties muffled like Arctic explorers. The only time when any of us had dared to take off our heavy overcoats, thick woollen scarves and fur gloves had been at the Arts on February 19 when the first part of *Back to Methuselah* had been revived, and a special dispensation obtained from the no-heating order for fear that otherwise the actor and actress playing Adam and Eve might perish of exposure.' They did not; audiences (and in general the London critics) remained rapt while Shaw piloted them down the long stream until Lilith (Frances Rowe) emerged from the dark with her noble valediction.

In 1947, five years after the re-opening, just over 30,000 people were paying annual subscriptions of five shillings, enabling them to buy reasonably-priced seats for themselves and guests. There were 4,500 full club members who (with an entrance fee of four guineas and a two-guinea annual subscription) could buy seats, use the lounge and bar, and dine until midnight in the restaurant. Lively, appreciative, and loyal, these members could have been grateful for their year. Thus, before the pentateuch, Frederick Valk, most overwhelmingly concentrated of actors, had appeared as Ibsen's John Gabriel Borkman. Later, Norman Marshall directed Simon Gantillon's *Maya,* haunted play of harlotry in dockside Marseilles. The year included Reginald Beckwith's *Boys in*

Brown, about a group of dead-end kids, also directed by Marshall; as well as a minor revival of Denis Johnston's *The Moon in the Yellow River,* a study of Ireland (fanatics and playboys), with one frightening theatrical stroke.

A more than useful year, then, and one that maintained the repertory system London had desired. A fresh excitement loomed. Christopher Fry, the theatre's resident dramatist, had written a new verse play; those who had a chance to read his rough script—cyclostyled pages that seemed to ignite in the hand—were certain that the spring of 1948, and *The Lady's Not for Burning,* would be the Arts at its meridian. It was. Clunes, who had not acted on his stage for eighteen months or more, had found in *The Lady* a part that—with Sir Harry Wildair— would stand first among everything he did in Great Newport Street.

1   It did have a production (which must have derived from the Agate-
    Clunes debate) at the Intimate Theatre, Palmers Green, in December
    1944, directed by Ronald Kerr—to avoid confusion we use 'directed'
    instead of the then customary 'produced'—and with Donald Strachan,
    Ernest Haines, Jean Webster Brough, David Stringer and Chris Castor in
    the company.
2   J.C. Trewin: *Peter Brook: A Biography* (Macdonald, 1971), p. 17.
3   *Sunday Times,* 14.10.1945; reprinted in *The Contemporary Theatre 1944 and
    1945* (Harrap, 1946), pp. 226–8.
4   *Peter Brook,* p. 28.
5   *Anything for a Quiet Life* (Elm Tree Books, 1973), p. 82.
6   *Six Thousand and One Nights* (Harrap, 1960), p. 212.

CHAPTER FOUR
'THE LADY' AND AFTER: 1948–1950

The year 1948 began with Jean-Jacques Bernard's delicate *Invitation to a Voyage*. After this, Richard Hughes' Welsh folk-piece, *A Comedy of Good and Evil;* and then, on the night of March 10, directed by Jack Hawkins, *The Lady's Not For Burning*. As Fry was to put it in a preface to the printed text, *The Lady* was 'an approximately medieval comedy', a 'comedy of human intelligences in a dance together... The comedy is a climate, of damp and dry, of spirit and matter, playing April with each other, and the climate is the comedy'. The important word is 'dance', for Fry taught dramatic poetry to dance again. Long before his arrival most dramatists had dreaded 'poetic' language in the theatre; they were as reserved as their actors were diffident. Suddenly, with little warning—maybe the *Phoenix* should have been a hint—we reached *The Lady* which, over the years, would be the first of four mood-plays of the seasons[1] (this was Spring), their language flashing like a heliograph in sunlight. Fry had a good time while he was working. 'As I remember it,' he wrote to the present authors, 'the general atmosphere was delightful. I certainly enjoyed it, both the work and the rehearsing, and the meeting with people, Club members, in the bar and restaurant.' Clunes had recognised that the play—which did not depend upon its narrative— was restoring verse drama to a stage that had long neglected it. At once, though knowing that the Arts might lose on the experiment, he and his advisers took the risk of doing it, himself as Thomas Mendip, the man who wants to be hanged, and Sheila Manahan as the girl, Jennet Jourdemayne, a suspected witch, who does not want to be burned. Aware that an audience might be puzzled during the first twenty minutes or so until it was in the spirit of the verse with its glistening fall of imagery, Clunes warned the cast that if, by then, there was no response, above all things the pace should not be quickened; if anything it should be slower. His prediction was reasonable. Phrases now familiar (such as Mendip's 'I'm a black and frosted rosebud whom the good God has preserved since last October') had the house in silent surprise. Pace was reduced; laughter began to come, and at the end of the night the cheering went on and on.

This was the company:

Richard	Derek Blomfield
Thomas Mendip	Alec Clunes
Alizon Eliot	Daphne Slater
Nicholas Devize	Michael Gough
Margaret Devize	Henzie Raeburn
Humphrey Devize	Gordon Whiting
Hebble Tyson	Andrew Leigh
Jennet Jourdemayne	Sheila Manahan
Chaplain	Frank Napier
Edward Tappercoom	Peter Bull
Matthew Skipps	Morris Sweden

Clunes had the humorous irony and imaginative vision for the discharged soldier, Mendip. Sheila Manahan's Jennet could not wholly match him; but three performances in that first cast linger still: Frank Napier's frail Chaplain, Peter Bull's Tappercoom ('I am not a nervous man/But I like to be predisposed to an order of events'), and Daphne Slater as the girl Alizon ('Coming in from the light, I am all out at the eyes... I've an April blindness').

At this period Clunes' attitude to his own performances was a puzzle. For a substantial period he had preferred not to act at all, but to spend his time either in and around the Arts or, as a dilettante, searching for theatre books of which he had a great many, and contemplating a secondary career as a dealer. Occasionally he would direct a play. But no one could depend upon his reaction at a given moment. He would either take months off, as on the Continental tour, playing a trinity of exacting parts, or he would be out altogether.

Not really lazy, not really a dilettante, he believed that he ought not to act too often. It might be argued, so he said, that he was running the theatre for himself. Yet, whenever box-office returns began to dip perilously, Wordsworth would suggest that it could be the hour to choose a part. Often reluctantly, he would, and the box-office moved with him. Mendip he could not resist. Moreover, here the direction was mainly his. Jack Hawkins, who had the programme credit, principally directed Clunes' own scenes. Alec would have liked, at heart, to do Mendip in the West End but he had to be cautious. Several managers, at first politely interested in West End rights, would not take them; too dangerous (wiseacres thought) in what used to be known as the prevailing climate.

This did not last. Presently John Gielgud was at home from touring in the United States with *Love for Love* and *The Importance of Being Earnest* and playing three or four parts in New York. What did he think of *The*

Lady? He declared himself without pause. On a rail journey to Cambridge with Hugh ('Binkie') Beaumont, master-mind of the West End firm, H.M. Tennent, Gielgud read the first act and told Beaumont on the spot: 'You must get this play for me'.[2] Beaumont did so, though for several reasons—among them a sagging revival of Hankin's *The Return of the Prodigal*—it took a year to set up a West End production, at the Globe in Shaftesbury Avenue. There Gielgud was Mendip; Pamela Brown, Jennet; and a single survivor from the original cast, Peter Bull, Tappercoom. Gielgud (as Clunes knew) would be the draw, and his decision ensured valuable royalties to the Arts down the years. *The Lady* ran for 294 performances, as well as for 156 in New York.

When, during May 1948, after his Arts Mendip, Clunes accepted a West End part, he chose curiously to appear as Robert Browning in a second-rate Garrick Theatre revival of Rudolf Besier's *The Barretts of Wimpole Street* that looked in grief from the start. He did have a reason, for transiently he was infatuated with Margaret Johnston (the Elizabeth Barrett; none could have been better). But in this piece immense responsibility rests upon the tyrannous father Edward Moulton-Barrett, created by Cedric Hardwicke, and the backers, even with H.K. Ayliff to direct, had cast—of all people—Tom Walls, for many years the galloping majors of Aldwych farce and now lamentably mis-matched. The production died. Clunes was back at the Arts where he neither acted nor directed until December. Peter Powell at this time was director for the Great Newport Street Committee, the management's official title.

Three years after the war, with membership still advancing, the Arts looked unshakeable. Its club was even more of a rendezvous; for critics the monthly change of play would be almost invariably fruitful. It was a paradox that, practically at the centre of the West End, the Arts should be technically on the outer circle, as a short-run theatre. It had companions in the 'Q', now among the oldest survivors; the Mercury at Notting Hill that had sheltered poets' plays in a world suspicious of them; the New Lindsey, also at Notting Hill, in effect a large room seating 162; the toiling Chepstow and Gateway, over in Bayswater; the minute Torch, curiously like a 'bus-top', up a winding stair in Wilton Place, Knightsbridge; the Left-wing Unity in a street near King's Cross; the Embassy in an inner surburban road at Swiss Cottage; the ambitious mayfly of the Boltons in South Kensington; and the Lyric, Hammersmith, behind market-barrows off Hammersmith Broadway. But none of these insisted, as the Arts did, that the Theatre had an exciting past as well as a present, and that it was wasteful to let the prized work of other periods wither, neglected, on the shelf.

During the remainder of 1948 the Arts had a customary

programme, even if it did nothing comparable to *The Lady.* Shaw took his customary airing, at first with *Major Barbara* by the Western Theatre Company, Barbara Lott showing the metal for her namesake. Resuming a flirtation with the Norwegian dramatist, Helge Krog, one of Clunes' pleasures, Sonia Dresdel, Robert Harris, and André Morell gave a conscientious performance of a dull conscientious play, *Break-Up.* A revival, after seventeen years, of Ronald Mackenzie's *Musical Chairs* followed it.

So, in July, to the latest Festival. This covered six productions—seven, if you counted a Gogol curtain-raiser—within five months: the dramatists were Ibsen (*Rosmersholm*), Shaw (*Too True To Be Good*), under the Shavian specialist, Esme Percy; Chekhov, Molière, Gogol (two plays), Verneuil: unquestionably Clunes' International Theatre. Before the opening, and indeed while *Rosmersholm* was still in rehearsal and Fanny Taylor working on her imaginative sets, Guy Sheppard supervised the theatre's re-decoration and (with several new seats) the re-carpeting of the auditorium.

A useful Festival beginning; but the plays themselves, in which Marius Goring and his wife Lucie Mannheim had most to do and did it with unabated resource and urgency, seldom heightened the pulse-beat. There were troubles. Thus Lord Longford's text of *Tartuffe* reduced Molière to frequent jingles ('With something of your father's right dispense/And force me not to this obedience'); and the production thrust 1664 into the visual styles of 1948, steel furniture and all. In spite of intelligent acting, the chosen method simply wiped the bloom from a great comedy. In *The Cherry Orchard* Daphne Slater (Anya) and Stanley van Beers (the forsaken manservant Firs) had Chekhovian quality; otherwise, apart from a few speeches by Wilfrid Walter as the landowner Pishtchik, it was a night of high intentions gone adrift. The final production was the best, Verneuil's three-act duologue with telephonic interludes, *The Third Man;* Lucie Mannheim as the bride with a past who weaves a skein of lies for her artist-bridegroom (Marius Goring) in their Montmartre flat.

That Christmas Alec Clunes was acting again, having discovered in James Bridie's *Gog and MacGog* a part he vastly enjoyed. Bridie himself, twinkling through a curtain-speech, said that his comedy was a 'piece of Scotch mist', and Clunes at the heart of the mist invented a kind of Doric Laneworthy-Figg. Possibly the label was unfair, for he worked more subtly, finding a quick stabbing pathos besides giving to the itinerant poet a roll in the voice, a gleam in the eye, and a whirling fury of declamation like the most eloquent windmill in 'the Hither Highlands'. (The inspiration might have been MacGonagall; nobody denied it.) Bravely, Esme Percy contrived to direct.

Clunes, who never ceased to love the late Victorian period, had his fun with it as director early in 1949. The play was Sydney Grundy's *A Pair of Spectacles,* renowned in 1890 for the part John Hare created and Denys Blakelock revived now: an amiable personage, Benjamin Goldfinch, who had merely to assume his hard-fisted brother's spectacles to become a domestic Scrooge. At the Arts David Bird acted the brother with a gritty pleasure, as of a steam-roller plumping damp gravel; but the night had to be Blakelock's in his relishing alternation of benevolently throbbing cat-in-cream goodwill with the teasiest misanthropy. Princess Margaret, who had been a few months before to the première of Gogol's *Marriage,* arrived on the first night to sit in the front row of the dress circle with a party of twelve.

Grundy's piece hardly resembled its successor, also late-Victorian, Shaw's *Widowers' Houses,* his first play and one (so he said) that made him 'infamous' as a dramatist. By 1949 it was a collectors' jewel. Though its opening audience was tepid, the narrative of slum landlords, municipal jobbery and 'tainted' money seemed to be entirely actable, and a critic observed in *Punch:*[3] 'Shakespearians look on in envy. Won't someone have a shot at, say, *Titus Andronicus?*' (There would not be long to wait.) GBS, who seldom failed to applaud the Arts, hastened to send his latest photograph, behind the ornamental gate of Shaw's Corner at Ayot St. Lawrence, and captioned 'The Old Widower in his House'. After these weeks of rhetoric it was probably a good idea to go on to *The Unquiet Spirit* (directed by John Fernald) from Jean-Jacques Bernard's Theatre of Silence, a wistful pastel drawing, with Margaret Rawlings and Richard Wordsworth as the two people who are destined for each other, but who can never quite achieve a meeting. Then another rediscovery, Somerset Maugham's mid-period *Caroline,* a comedy that preserved an ingratiating good temper, nothing acid or acrid.

It was a consistent year. Having tried an amiable but over-praised American piece, James Thurber and Elliott Nugent's *The Male Animal,* later transferred to the New Theatre for a brief run, the Arts went back to Clunes' favourite Edwardian bran-tub: this promptly provided Hubert Henry Davies' four-in-hand, *The Mollusc* (1907) about the limp, clinging woman—Vivienne Bennett in Mary Moore's part—who devotes her energy to getting other people to work for her (which they do). Back further yet to the more-or-less roaring Eighties and Pinero's farce, *The Schoolmistress,* not so majestically funny as *The Magistrate,* though the straight-faced zeal with which John Fernald directed did not overlook the chatty fireman ready in mid-blaze with any number of superfluous Good Stories. Still, the famous and unforgotten lines would be 'It is an embarrassing thing to break a bust in the house of comparative strangers' and the description of a small pork-pie as 'architecturally disproportionate'. Remaining plays until Christmas were minor. Clunes, acting for once, could not do a lot with a designing young man who battens on the Moscow society of 1860 in Rodney Ackland's version of *The Diary of a Scoundrel:* a piece with plenty of dramatic fuel that failed to take fire, possibly because the cast was working too hard for its laughter.

Before leaving the autumn of 1949 we have to remember *Hindle Wakes,* the play by Stanley Houghton that Clunes, a steady admirer, directed wisely: he was fortunate enough to have as his leading actor Herbert Lomas, standing six feet and more—and known to the profession as 'Tiny'—as Nat Jeffcote, the part he had created nearly forty years earlier for the Horniman company in Manchester. Unexampled in his vein, gaunt and weathered, his voice sounding like a winter wind across the Pennines, Lomas had with him such members of the old guard as Eileen Thorndike and Milton Rosmer. Strangely, Arts audiences seemed to treat the piece as a discovery: in both intervals at the première people were debating it with so much heat and what-can-happen-next argument that anybody uninstructed might have mistaken it for a new prize of contemporary drama. If ever a revival needed immediate transference to the official West End, this was it; every second notice said so. But nothing happened.

Clunes, who had been married in August 1949 to the actress Stella Richman—a marriage that did not last—appeared to be gradually lessening his work at the Arts. During the early autumn of 1950 he went back to what he called his 'cradle' at the Old Vic for an exacting season: Orsino, Waspe in *Bartholomew Fair,* Henry V, Ford in *The Merry Wives of Windsor.* For a time John Fernald, among the busiest theatre-men of the period, and Roy Rich, comparably versatile and ready, shared the tasks of artistic director.

With occasional visits South, Fernald had spent three packed years at the Liverpool Playhouse. Glad to be in London, one of his first Arts plays under the new system was a fastidious recreation of Eleanor Farjeon's fantasy, *The Silver Curlew,* which he had done at Liverpool in 1948. In effect, an East Anglian gloss on the Rumpelstiltskin story, and wittily scored by Clifton Parker (two pianos, drums, and singers), it is a blend of nursery-matter and fantasy without twitching into the weaker whimsy. It ought to have entered the short list of Christmas annuals.

Except for two productions by Clunes and one by Max Adrian, direction during 1950 was split almost evenly between Fernald (five plays) and Rich (four). Though he had heard—and it was true enough—that Clunes could be despotic when he wished, Fernald got on with him easily; he would never blame his directors for any mistakes, and he let them have a free choice of play. The alternation with Rich worked helpfully, for each could have four weeks' rehearsal time for the month's run. Fernald's opening play in 1950 (the Norwegian Ambassador at the première) was *John Gabriel Borkman* in an excellently speakable version by himself and his wife, Jenny Laird; they had worked on a preliminary literal text, which like many other literal texts could be very funny at times, for three concentrated weeks in Cornwall. Borkman, near-Napoleonic, was the kind of thundercloud that the Czech actor, Frederick Valk, could make fiercely impressive. Almost every notice that counted was superb: for Fernald's production as well as for Valk's relentless drive, his control of the miner's son, obsessed and doomed, who worships the metal that sings in the earth. T.C. Worsley,[4] drama critic of the *New Statesman,* commented upon 'a happy resemblance to Ibsen himself', the stocky figure, the full face, the rocky chin. Certainly an event, even if some audiences, less prepared than others, could not endure the unremitting tension, and Valk had once or twice to quell them with a look.

During the spring of 1950 the theatre's Shaw prize for the best new play by a British dramatist performed there during the previous twelve months went to *Gog and MacGog:* it had been so successful that Clunes had thought of re-naming it gratefully, *Bless the Bridie.* Generously, the dramatist returned his prize and doubled the amount (£100). It was now that the Arts announced its second new-play competition: £500 for the best full-length entry with a 'theme of contemporary significance'—the same qualification as earlier—submitted by November 1; the winner to be staged during the Festival of Britain. Judges: Alec Clunes, Christopher Fry, Peter Ustinov. There would be unguessed breakers ahead.

1   The others were: (Summer) *A Yard of Sun,* Nottingham Playhouse and
      Old Vic, 1970; (Autumn) *Venus Observed,* St. James's, 1950; and (Winter)
      The Dark Is Light Enough, Aldwych, 1954.
2   John Gielgud: *An Actor and his Time* (Sidgwick & Jackson, 1979),
      p. 162.
3   *Punch* (J.C.T.), 16.2.1949.
4   *The New Statesman,* 11.3.1950.

CHAPTER FIVE
ALL THE SAINTS: 1950-1952

Maybe a robust and over-valued Restoration comedy was not exactly the relief needed after *Borkman*. Max Adrian directed Vanbrugh's *The Provok'd Wife* without much style apart from the conventional matters of snuff-taking and handkerchief-waving. The next play, Chekhov's *Ivanov,* was a happy change, and Fernald, a Chekhov specialist, treated it sympathetically in a version by J.P. Davis. Faultier than the masterpieces of a decade later, it has its own beauties and humours, and the Ivanov, Michael Hordern, not widely known in those days, never slackened his grasp. He had presence, personality, voice. He projected himself; he was unafraid to move, and he phrased his monologues with the subtlest balance. Round him was much appreciative playing: Helen Shingler's pathos as the dying wife, Helena Pickard's bounce-and-chatter as the woman who would like to be a Countess, Frederick Leister's method of smoothing along a kind old drunkard, and in particular the astonishing husk of a man that Hugh Pryse made of a little angry-grasshopper Count once acted by Stanislavsky. Fernald was proud that in *Ivanov* he gave a first chance to Alec McCowen, thanks to the recommendation of an actress at Liverpool who asked if he could see a young man she had been with in repertory. Cast for the tiny part of a guest who arrives late and who finds nothing to eat or drink, McCowen had only about ten lines; he got a laugh on every one.

The Arts was coming now to its hundredth production since the new order of 1942. Clunes had wondered about presenting *Man and Superman* in full; he had acted the Juan-in-Hell episode so often that he felt it might be pleasant (and forgivable) to wrap the rest of the piece around him. But glumly, and at the twelfth hour, Shaw, who had usually given the Arts what it asked for, refused consent because an American director wanted a revival. That sounded like a flimsy excuse. No matter; Clunes, accepting it, decided to do *Macbeth,* a plan that worried a number of people, not least (theatre-folk are unconscionably superstitious) because of its reputation as a 'haunted' play and a fear that the celebration might be disastrous. Never this, it was indifferently received. As with the Arts *Hamlet,* it had to be a pocket edition. Clunes, his own director, approached it sensibly, resolving—unlike many

Macbeths—not to hurtle at the early scenes and to have no strength left for the banquet and its terrors or for Dunsinane and the last despair. Even so, it was too often unexciting. Adept Shakespearian that he had become, Clunes was not in the Macbeth mould, though admirable in the shard-borne beetle and rooky-wood speeches when he looked from a great open window into the thickening twilight. Despite needless cuts and transpositions, the production, in its shaggy-craggy manner, did sometimes have a ring, and Clunes remembered Masefield's injunction:[1] 'Do not let your witches laugh. Satan's kingdom does not laugh.' Margaret Rawlings' Lady Macbeth, entirely intense, and the Macduff (Michael Hordern) were each commanding, yet the tragedy did not grow. Clunes, invariably self-critical as an actor, never felt right, and he would invariably admit it.

Undoubtedly the Arts was in its richer form when—turning its other cheek—it marked the ninety-fourth birthday of Bernard Shaw ('nothing exasperates me more than to be Georged in print') by reviving his 'fantasia in the Russian manner on English themes', *Heartbreak House;* the title speaks of 'cultured, leisured Europe', ostensibly before the war of 1914. With a prophetic fervour Walter Fitzgerald acted Shotover, the ancient who resembles a nautical Isaiah; and the whole company (Catherine Lacey's Hesione sparking in its midst) turned the night— which was also the 200th production of John Fernald's career—into as good a birthday present as Shaw would have wished. His prose is at its meridian; the second-act scene between Shotover and Ellie has more genuine poetry in it than much work determinedly metrical. Not four months later, in the mid-autumn of 1950, GBS died at Ayot St. Lawrence. No single English theatre since the Everyman had done what the Arts did to acclaim a writer who had taken the drama seriously as 'a factory of thought, a prompter of conscience, an elucidator of social conduct, an armoury against despair and dullness, and a Temple of the ascent of Man'.[2] Throughout life Clunes never faltered in his allegiance. (In 1959 he was happy to follow Rex Harrison as Higgins in the *Pygmalion* musical, *My Fair Lady,* at Drury Lane.)

The year swooped to its close with a lively set of plays that no London management could equal. From a young dramatist, Roger MacDougall's *The Gentle Gunman,* we can recall Robin Bailey trying to tell orthodox members of the I.R.A. why a policy of violence had to be futile. If, technically, not a major invention, it secured a stronger performance than several pieces constructionally perfect but ice-cold. Its dialogue stayed warm with argument; the cast spoke it with a similar warmth. The next Arts company, Brenda Bruce as the heroine Victoria, a 'dear little thing', frisked through Maugham's *Home and Beauty* which had a few weeks at the St. Martin's; John Fernald directed his father

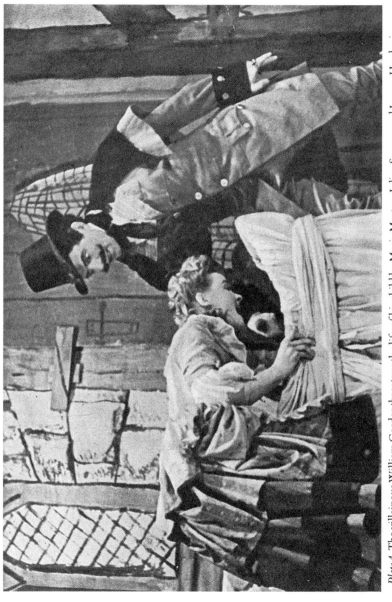

Plate 4. The villainous William Corder threatens the life of his child by Maria Marten. Julian Somers and Joanna Horder in Alec Clunes' first excursion into Victorian melodrama in October 1942. The set was by Maise Meiklejohn. (*B.B.C. Hulton Picture Library*)

Plate 5. Design by Jan Kurzke of Jenssen's *The Witch,* produced in Masefield's translation in February 1944. *(Photograph: Michael Kerr; Collection of Gillian Adams)*

C.B. Fernald's free version of Chiarelli's *The Mask and the Face;*
Catherine Lacey, in Hugh Ross Williamson's sober portrait, *Queen
Elizabeth,* was truthfully the Queen, not a contralto usurper; and,
continuing to preserve Pinero, the theatre recovered his all-but-lost
Preserving Mr. Panmure. Moderate stuff, but more to the taste of London
in 1950 than 1911, it went to the Aldwych with Gwen Cherrell and
Reginald Purdell as the governess and the man who kissed her. Joy
Parker, beautifully cast, was demurely the Lady Precious Stream of S.I.
Hsiung's irresistible Chinese charade.

It was the sharpest possible swerve to Jean Forbes-Robertson's
Hedda Gabler, one of her various appearances in the part and one that
would act itself into stage history. Past Heddas had overlooked the
dangerous humour; never merely baleful, she was resolved that we
should not forget, and nobody could have heard Hedda's mockery,
bitter as a distillation of poison-ivy, and bred of infinite boredom,
stressed as it was at the Arts. The emphasis did not harm the play; it is
inherent in the woman, a rapid flicker of mind and tongue. Jean Forbes-
Robertson wavered only in the burning of Lövborg's manuscript when
she turned theatrical and Hedda stiffened to pasteboard. (She must have
been grateful that the Gosse-and-Archer text did not drop to the literal
phrasing of a modern translation, 'It's now I am burning thy bairn,
Thea—I'm burning thy bairn now'.) Quickly in the last act she
recovered, helped by a judicious Brack: Campbell Singer sustained a
frigid suavity. One would not have thought, watching and hearing the
mocking sorceress with the contemptuous eyes and a voice that could
pounce and sear, that the same player was the definitive Peter Pan and
among the best Violas in memory.

Ibsen to Turgenev. Constance Cox's *Spring at Marino,* 'suggested'
by *Fathers and Sons,* emerged as a gentle sentimental comedy, a
fortnight's excursion in the country, with a rather watery text: it owed
everything to an observant production (Fernald's), with acting in key.
This was a pleasanter night than *Intimate Relations,* a new translation, by
Charles Frank, of Cocteau's *Les Parents Terribles* which suffered from
teething troubles. Fay Compton, the leading actress, said after a few
rehearsals that she would have to go if Kenneth Tynan, young,
opinionated, and not yet a drama critic, remained as director. The
ultimate victim was obvious; Clunes told William Wordsworth, who
had been used for many years to serving as a buffer, to break the news to
Tynan. Wordsworth did not think it was his job; eventually, after they
had tossed up for the dubious privilege, Brian Mellor, the Arts manager,
agreed to tell Tynan whom Judith Furse succeeded. The play,
apparently scrawled in grease-paint on a dressing-room mirror, drew
large audiences for five weeks, mainly owing to Fay Compton, Mary

Hinton, and Rosalie Crutchley as mother, aunt and mistress. At the Strand, where it reopened during the summer with a few cast changes, it was less successful.

This was the year of the Festival of Britain. Clunes, appearing as Henry V at the Old Vic, had not overlooked a festival for the Arts. It involved the production, within three months and in four consecutive programmes, of nearly all Shaw's brief plays, eighteen of them, from *The Man of Destiny* (1895) to *The Six of Calais* (1934): 100 parts, sixteen players, 150 costumes: a Topical Sketch Compiled from the Editorial and Correspondence Columns of the Daily Papers, A Disgrace to the Author, A Religious Tract in Dramatic Form, A Brief Tragedy for Barns and Booths, An Almost Historical Comedietta, A Piece of Utter Nonsense, A Recruiting Pamphlet, and a good deal else. Anybody able to put the right titles to these secondary descriptions could have marched into the Arts Theatre, beneath its special Festival-year canopy, with a real sense of pride. Unfortunately, the public took it less gratefully than Clunes had hoped; in fact, the festival lost what for the Arts was a lot of money, though the four programmes would have been a banquet for a minority of true believers; after a high summer under the dewdrops from the lion's mane, one visitor was heard to say that he had now met in performance Shaw's Complete Works with one exception: the full-length *Jitta's Atonement,* a perversion from a comedy by GBS's Austrian translator, Siegfried Trebitsch. (Curiously, this had been staged at the Arts as early as 1930.)

Village Wooing, the 'comediettina' for two voices, came out as well as anything. A footnote to *Man and Superman,* directed originally in England by Christopher Fry at the Pump Room, Tunbridge Wells, during 1934, we are not astonished when Z (who is a woman) captures A (who is a writer) at the final curtain: it may seem trivial, but at the Arts Brenda Bruce and Maurice Denham transformed it. Probably the most liked of the other plays were *Great Catherine,* with the 'liberal' Empress of Russia (Vivienne Bennett) at grips with a Captain Edstaston, of Spire View, Deepdene, Little Mugford, Devon, Shaw's eternal Briton; and the blank-verse parody, *The Admirable Bashville; or, Constancy Unrewarded,* which can flower into such a line as this: 'My cousin ails, Bashville. Procure some wet.' We were not sorry to have heard such loquacious trifles as *The Fascinating Foundling*—1909 was a year of Shavian fragments—or the nonsense of *Passion, Poison, and Petrifaction* with its stage direction (it must be read): 'A thunderbolt enters the room and strikes the helmet of the devoted constable whence it is attracted to the waistcoat of the doctor by the lancet in his pocket.' The Arts cast, with Rich, Fernald, Judith Furse, and Stephen Murray among the directors, offered through the months a collection of protean prodigies (one bill took three hours-and-a-half). It was a joy to listen to David Bird's voice, described variously as plum-and-syrup, satin-wrapped toffee, hot chocolate and a magnified purr. A most miraculous organ.

While the Shaw plays were halfway down the course, Alec Clunes announced the finalists for the Festival of Britain prize, now—plus £200 from the late James Bridie—standing at £700. There had been worries about the small number of entries, but before closing day scripts arrived pell-mell, the bulk of them during the last week. In the long run the judges (Clunes, Christopher Fry and Peter Ustinov) decided that three of a short-list of fifty (from 997) were of equal merit when read in manuscript; the choice must depend upon strength in performance. The trio, none written expressly for the competition, were Enid Bagnold's *Poor Judas,* C.E. Webber's *Right Side Up,* and John Whiting's *Saint's Day;* within a few months these dramatists became tangled in the most spirited theatrical argument for years, certainly in the record of the Arts Theatre.

Clunes planned to open in mid-July with Roy Rich's production of *Poor Judas,* a play about the treachery of one artist to another that had taken Enid Bagnold (characteristically) three years to write. At once wrath fell. Critics had never liked the idea of the competition, and though *Poor Judas* was far off the level track of playmaking, its author's wandering into literary thickets could not be condoned; it would be five years before her acknowledged triumph with *The Chalk Garden.* So that was that; critics having mourned at some length, waited for the second exhibit, *Right Side Up.* Before it arrived there was a frightening interlude. *Poor Judas* had almost ended its scheduled run when a fire that had possibly smouldered during afternoon and evening performances broke out in the orchestra pit forty minutes after Saturday's curtain-fall. Stacked furniture added to the flames which burned out the first four rows of stalls, damaged the ceilings, and put eighty per cent of the lighting equipment out of action. Clunes, who had gone on a Continental holiday, might have remained ignorant if he had not telegraphed from Bandol in the south of France, wishing success to the production. There were fifteen hotels in Bandol. Located by telephone at the seventh attempt, he hurried back.

The last Sunday performance of *Poor Judas* had been cancelled. It was impossible to get another theatre in time for *Right Side Up,* so Clunes told the cast: 'We open next Thursday. Let's get cracking!' Right away he began, aided by members of the company, the author (C.E. Webber) himself, stage-hands, typists, and actors from other theatres who had offered to help. Through the week-end they worked without break, clearing the debris and spraying with black paint sheets of scenery canvas sewn together to form an under-ceiling. Stage carpenters hammered together an orchestra pit to replace the old one that had been totally destroyed.

Punctually on Thursday, *Right Side Up* went on in the patched-up theatre. It ought to have been a winner if Fate were generous, but Fate was not. Like old Father William, the piece appeared to be standing on its head: the favourite posture of a wildly innocent 19-year-old 'tree-boy', a curious fellow who strayed into a gangster-flat in Soho, a kind of thieves' kitchen-cum-shooting gallery, to the alarm of all except the resident girl. The affair could be treated as a gangster-melodrama, as a parody of the gangster-play, as a fantasy, as an outbreak of symbolism. In any event, it was defiantly implausible. Ivor Brown said gloomily in *The Observer* (19.8.51): 'Had I been one of the hundreds of rejected competitors, I should have rubbed my eyes, or even gnashed a tooth, at finding *Right Side Up* put in the first three.' This was the general view. One play of the short-listed three remained, and critics (those who had not to linger at the Edinburgh Festival) waited for the night of September 5 and for John Whiting's *Saint's Day*.

Early that year John Whiting had had a group of friendly notices for his comedy, *A Penny for a Song*, at the Haymarket; a mild caprice, but there were grace and style in its ordering, and it made one regret that some writers damned it while allowing far cruder and rougher stuff free passage. It ran for just a month, yet it seemed to a cluster of optimists that there might be hope for Whiting and *Saint's Day*. At the time, no. It was greeted with derision. 'Of a badness,' said A.V. Cookman in *The Times* (6.9.51) 'that must be called indescribable.' Many other critics concurred (the most sympathetic would be in *John o'London's*).[3] Whereupon the judges, unheeding, awarded John Whiting the £700 prize with the citation: 'We welcome the arrival of a finely gifted dramatist and unhesitatingly recommend a visit to this exciting and stimulating play.'

Splendidly acted—nobody denied that—under Stephen Murray's direction, the play was about an old satirical poet and what happened to him at his country home on his 83rd birthday, January 25 (the anniversary of St. Paul's conversion). A bare statement of plot is useless: long afterwards, introducing the published text, Whiting wrote: 'The play took a little over two years to write. This may account for a Websterian accumulation of detail which has confused and angered many people. So much so that they often overlook the fact that the story is very simple. The theme... is self-destruction.' Michael Hordern's performance of Paul Southman is remembered now for its complete loyalty to the dramatist.

Notable figures—Peter Brook and Tyrone Guthrie, Peggy Ashcroft and John Gielgud—protested against the serried criticism.

Plate 6. Maise Meiklejohn's design for the Inn Scene of *Leonce and Lena* (February 1945).
(*Photograph: Michael Kerr; Collection of Michael Warre*)

Plate 7. Setting for O'Neill's *Anna Christie* (November 1944), one of Jan Kurzke's most successful designs for the Arts.
(Photograph: Michael Kerr; Collection of Gillian Adams)

Plate 8. Christopher Fry's first popular success, *A Phoenix Too Frequent,* directed for the Arts by Noel Willman in November 1946, with Paul Scofield as Tegeus, the Corporal, and Joan White as the maid Doto. The comedy had originally been staged at the Mercury in April that year.
(*Photograph: John Vickers; Collection of Mrs. Clunes*)

Plate 9. Michael Warre's models of his transportable settings for *Hamlet* (1945 and 1947).
Top left: the Platform;
top right: the Throne Room;
centre: Clunes as Hamlet on the continental tour of 1947;
bottom left: the Churchyard;
bottom right: Forestage Scenes.
(*Collection of Michael Warre*)

THE GOSPEL OF THE BROTHERS BARNABAS

MICHAEL WARRE 1945

Plate 10. Set by Michael Warre for Part 2 of Shaw's "metabiological pentateuch", *Back to Methuselah*, "The Gospel of the Brothers Barnabas". This was staged in its entirety at the Arts between February and April 1947 and has not since been mounted in London. (*Photograph: Michael Kerr; Collection of Michael Warre*)

Plate 11. The original Arts production of Fry's *The Lady's not for Burning*, with (left to right) Derek Blomfield (Richard), Andrew Leigh (Hebble Tyson), Alec Clunes (Thomas Mendip) and Henzie Raeburn (Margaret Devize). Performed at the Arts in March 1948, it was May 1949 before it reached the West End with John Gielgud and Pamela Brown in the leading roles. *(Photograph: Angus McBean)*

Plate 12. Alec Clunes, Golda Casimir and Gwen Bacon in Rodney Ackland's dramatisation of Ostrovsky's *Diary of a Scoundrel* (October 1949). (*Photograph: Angus McBean; Collection of Mrs Clunes*)

George Devine[4] claimed in *The Radio Times:* 'To me it splits wide open the conventional forms of playwriting and allies itself with the other modern arts in a way that no other play has done. It helps the theatre to bridge the gap of time which exists between itself and other forms of artistic expression. Such a play cannot be dismissed as an oddity without much future. Indeed, I believe we shall find that it is one of the first clear signs to the future.' (This was five years before the theatre 'rebellion' of 1956.)

Alec Clunes had responded serenely to the attack (and he could not have guessed then how prophetically he spoke): '*Saint's Day* may have been knocked. The public may even have been puzzled. But in twenty years' time you will know why I was not disappointed.' On September 17, 1951, he wrote to Christopher Fry: 'Dear Christopher, I am delighted to say that *Saint's Day,* though a considerable way from paying for itself, is doing increasingly good business and that I have had a fine crop of letters;† about fifty per cent of them have been as angrily appreciative as the remaining fifty per cent have been angrily critical, and an increasing number of intelligent bodies have been either 'phoning or speaking to me here. I am very glad indeed that we did the piece and think that, however much it may cost us in simple pennies, it has proved *very* much worth-while from all the other points of view. Yours sincerely, ALEC.

†P.S. Cecil Day Lewis most profusely appreciative.'

Addressing the Royal Society of Literature (17.10.63) Christopher Fry said: '*Saint's Day* stands... as close to a masterpiece as almost any first play has come.' Today, more than three decades after the Arts première, it is honoured for what it is, uneven, exciting, provocative, an experiment far in advance of its time, a wild landscape of the mind.

Gradually, in the autumn of 1951, the debate tired itself out and critics and audiences settled comfortably to the next production, an unassuming revival of another of Maugham's comedies from his Edwardian heyday. *Mrs. Dot* (in the modes of 1908) was about a brewer's charming widow, with £60,000 a year, who used feminine strategy to get the man she wanted, and in the course of this mirrored the Edwardian round, the unclouded run of house-parties, the vast incomes, the troops of servants. Not another *Smith,* the piece did work. Nothing in it resembled its successor, an American dramatist Andrew Rosenthal's intelligent *Third Person,* which had a touch, if less explicit, of *The Green Bay Tree.* A young man named Kip had become a sort of parasitic growth in the New York home of a war-time companion; now and again, not so much a play as a case-history, it managed to be soundly dramatic, though there was a superfluity of portentous suggestion and too many canakins were clinked; the young man had Denholm Elliot's special tautness. The Arts had to retain it for a fifth week; and at length, with a few alterations, the Lord Chamberlain—who had firmly banned its appearance outside a club theatre—permitted a transference to the Criterion. It was unlucky that the new management insisted, in the manner of the time, upon labelling *Third Person* as 'an adult play'.

A forty-year-old comedy by Arnold Bennett was the last engagement during an Arts year that could have shared in its title, *The Great Adventure.* Bennett had a potentially fruitful notion, used first in his novel, *Buried Alive,* when he thought of Ilam Carve, an eminent (and shy) artist who was quite willing, as the chance served, for his valet to be buried in his stead in Westminster Abbey while he found peace for himself out at Putney. Maurice Denham (artist; a part created by Henry Ainley) and Jenny Laird (a protective widow amiably christened Janet Cannot) had to work to bear off the night. But, in a Fernald production, they managed it, taking the Arts, already with another ambitious adventure in hand, to the early weeks of 1952. It was now the tenth year since what began as 'the Arts Group of Actors' had restored the theatre uncannily at the height, or depth, of the war.

1   *A Macbeth Production* (Heinemann, 1945), p. 34.
2   From Shaw's preface (*The Author's Apology*) written in 1906 for a selection from his criticisms (*Dramatic Opinions and Essays*) edited in America by James Huneker. It is reprinted in Volume 1 of *Our Theatres in the Nineties* (Constable, 1932), p. 7.
3   *John o' London's Weekly,* 28.9.1951 ('Questions About a Prizewinner').
4   *Radio Times,* 5.10.1951.

CHAPTER SIX
WINTER GARDEN: 1952

The Winter Garden Theatre, no longer a name, is not even a legend like the St. James's. In spite of early hilarities in musical comedy between the wars, and, intermittently, a few long runs later, it never managed to be a household word for the specialist or the general playgoer. (The New London is now on the site.) There had been high days, it is true; the comedian Leslie Henson, with his squeezed-lemon face, acted at the Winter Garden for seven years, 1919–1926, beginning with *Kissing Time,* after the building in Drury Lane, previously the New Middlesex Theatre of Varieties, had been re-opened and redecorated by the Grossmith and Laurillard management. It would grow into an ever-ready house used, without overriding policy, for such productions as musicals, Shaw's *On the Rocks,* Donald Wolfit in Shakespeare—he was Iago to Frederick Valk's Othello—and Joan Temple's blistering 'evacuee' drama, *No Room at the Inn.*

At the New Year of 1952 it was vacant. It held about 1640 people with an unusually spacious gallery. Drama critics thought of it as a rather dim cavern, the place where sham icicles hung by the auditorium wall. Not particularly attractive, then, and what had it to do with the Arts, a club theatre one-fifth the size? In the cold spring of 1952, a great deal. For months—even while *Saint's Day* was running—people at the Arts had debated the possibility of a companion theatre, somewhere in which to expand. The Rank Organisation had been trying to sell the Winter Garden, freed now from Christmas-holiday matinees of *Where the Rainbow Ends.* Hence the altruistic plan in Great Newport Street: to lease it and turn it under a non-profit-distributing company (no entertainments tax) into a 'people's theatre' for which anyone might buy a seat: half-a-guinea (52½p) as the top price, against the West End average of 14s (70p), and five hundred seats at two shillings (10p) each.

Most of the money for the scheme would derive from the transference of Arts successes, especially *The Lady's Not For Burning;* thus it was natural to choose Fry's early play, *The Firstborn,* much revised, and with a new third act since the original première at Edinburgh. Looking forward to space at last, Clunes said he hoped to follow this with five- or six-week runs of *The Constant Couple* (Wildair again), *The Merchant of*

Venice, and—if the omens were favourable—Otway's seldom-revived *Venice Preserv'd.* 'No play that gets to grips with modern problems,' the *Daily Worker* commented sourly.[1] Llewellyn Rees, formerly drama director of the Arts Council, later administrator of the Old Vic, was appointed to control the project. 'His presence at the club during the last few weeks has been very noticeable' said a member of the Arts staff, to which the *Daily Telegraph* added a note: 'I imagine, a considerable understatement.'[2]

Advance bookings did seem hopeful. On January 29, while E.M. Delafield's *To See Ourselves* held the Arts stage, up in mid-Drury Lane the Winter Garden curtain rose on *The Firstborn,* directed by John Fernald, set by Michael Warre, and with Alec Clunes as Moses, the young man slowly aware of his tremendous mission in the Deliverance, the Israelite struggle against Pharaoh during the summer of the seven plagues of Egypt. It was a grand first night (and at 1914 prices). Fry proved how a poet-dramatist could transform an apparently intractable theme; re-shaping his original work, he had sacrificed neither passion nor theatrical power. Clunes was superbly dominating, a man wrenched between his nature and his accepted destiny, but fit to receive the Commandments upon Sinai; the mouthpiece of the Lord God of Israel. With him were such players as Mark Dignam, the rigid man unable to forget that he is the Pharaoh, Seti the Second, King of Upper and Lower Egypt, Lord of the Two Lands; Barbara Everest, Tony Britton, and (as a young apostate-Jew) Robert Rietty.

Notices were splendid, yet the play did not animate the box-office. Whatever the cause, the Biblical theme or the unfamiliarity of the Winter Garden, audiences during six weeks of a frigid spring were regrettably poor. There would have to be a final throw. At the Arts *The Constant Couple* had been a double-six; repeat that at the Winter Garden and all might yet be well. Meantime the Arts season had continued with Jean Anouilh's *Thieves' Carnival,* a translation (by Lucienne Hill) of *Le Bal des Voleurs;* it stayed until its end a mild-ballet-comedy, a fascination, an early *pièce rose* during which three pickpockets, confidence tricksters in a French spa, raised their own castle in Spain.

The March revival of *The Constant Couple,* the third in which Clunes had appeared, was London's first public performance since Drury Lane in 1805. The Winter Garden stage had been extended into the house to resemble, as nearly as possible, the stage of a Restoration theatre. Fanny Taylor again designed the decor. 'If *The Constant Couple* is not back at its old home,' Clunes wrote in the programme, 'it has at least come back to the same street.' Instinctively aware that the venture rested upon this, most drama critics joined the rescue party. A.V. Cookman (*The Times*)[3] did feel that in the wide acreage of the Winter

Garden the dialogue was unduly amplified, but he added that Clunes had returned with consistent grace to his imperturbable, humorous beau: 'He brings to the drunken courtship a spirit of good humour which purifies, or at any rate intensifies, its humour to the point at which there is no resisting it.' This was the era of a Sunday radio-discussion, 'The Critics'. Discussing *The Constant Couple,* the group found itself at odds, Philip Hope-Wallace and C.V. Wedgwood strongly for the play, C.A. Lejeune acknowledging that it contained at least two good lines—she did not say which—and Tom Hopkinson suggesting (a little late) that there should have been music.

For all the publicity, the run lasted only six weeks; the season expired after twelve. Wisely, the lease had contained a clause that allowed Clunes to withdraw if box-office support failed to justify continuance. He remained gallant, saying that he hoped to restart at the same theatre in the autumn, but if he were frank with himself he knew that there was never any hope of this. 'We haven't paid our way as we expected to, we haven't a lot of money behind us, and at present it would be unwise to carry on.' So, on April 20, Wildair uttered his disbelieving 'Woof!' for the last time. It was back to the Arts where *Uncle Vanya* had finished a month's run and an Indian dancer was filling in while Fernald rehearsed Granville-Barker's Edwardian play, *The Voysey Inheritance.*

J.P. Davis, a Birkenhead income-tax official—obviously news for the gossip columns—had translated all the major work of Chekhov, a dramatist with whom Fernald, as director, was usually at ease. But for once, with *Uncle Vanya,* his flair momentarily weakened. The production, said the *New Statesman,* suggested how beautiful the play could be without reaching the heart of it. Jenny Laird's Sonya was as sensitive as courageous, but Cyril Luckham blurred Vanya, and John Justin's Astrov, man of the trees, needed more time for ripening.

Immediately after *Vanya* members of the Critics' Circle met in an upper room of the Arts for an unaccustomed purpose: to hear Christopher Fry speak, with charm and candour, on 'An Experience of Critics'.[4] He talked of the competition that bred *Saint's Day;* the only time he had felt that the whole critical profession had chosen to use only one eye. Eloquently, he defended *Saint's Day:* '...Very often a dramatic economy which presented in a few lines what would take many dramatists half an act: a sense conveyed of a haunted world, haunted by human beings unable to understand themselves or each other, haunted by fear of life, by the wooing of the powers of death, haunted by will-lessness and lack of love... Then the question of the play's obscurity, and there is no question: it is obscure. It is obscure, that is to say, to the brain. It is not, I think, at all obscure to the nerves. It is obscure if we must always know where we are. It is not obscure if we think it good sometimes to ask "Where are we?" It is obscure and not obscure as a man's self is obscure and not obscure. It is when the characters seemed about to address themselves to our brains, or when we seemed to come up against a devised symbolism, that the play became untrue to itself.'

Down in the theatre the next production was John Fernald's again, but with a cast little beyond serviceable (Hugh Miller and Tony Britton most authentic). When in 1905 Granville-Barker wrote *The Voysey Inheritance* on the theme of absolute honesty, Shaw was lord of the Court Theatre, and Barker disappoints us by smudging the purely theatrical quality of his drama and turning it to a Shavian conversation-piece. Yet, at the last, we know the Voyseys backward; few stage families are so amply drawn. It was imaginative of the Arts to restore the piece and in what Ivor Brown[5] called 'full Edwardian canonicals', with 'a wonderful dining-room' (Eric Keown)[6] 'that at every point, from chandelier to stained-glass window, awakes nostalgic pangs'. The designer was Paul Mayo.

On to still another revival—disgruntled playgoers had not considered the value of true repertory— this time to Harold Brighouse's *Hobson's Choice*. David Bird, always vocally prodigal, endowed Henry Horatio Hobson with a voice that contrived to hint at lumpy porridge and a wet Salford morning, while Pauline Jameson's resolutely feminist Maggie was the salt in the porridge. Donald Pleasence kept Mossop, single or married, within bounds. All said, a likeable gift for a birthday, Clunes' tenth as theatre director of the Arts: a night of many happy returns, and good news from the box-office.

1   *Daily Worker*, 28.12.1951.
2   *Daily Telegraph*, 21.12.1951.
3   *The Times*, 15.3.1952.
4   *An Experience of Critics* (Penguin, 1952), p. 20.
5   *Observer*, 11.5.1952.
6   *Punch*, 21.5.1952.

CHAPTER SEVEN
BIRTHDAY: 1952-1953

For those trained in a repertory audience, the ardours and endurances of weekly-change long ago, or the luxury of monthly runs (as at Barry Jackson's Birmingham), Alec Clunes' method made theatrical sense. A choice of new work, of course, when possible, but a repertory theatre, first of all, should be a place of revival, of preservation. Alec Clunes did not restrict the Arts stage to his national findings. He went abroad, to France and Norway, America, Russia, Spain: the Arts was a small international house that never played down to its consistently loyal public. If it could not keep the same people together—an original ideal of the Arts Group of Actors—its casts were thoroughly professional; rising players had chances in Great Newport Street they could not get elsewhere.

Inevitably ('I expect to put on the plays I like') the Arts would speak through Clunes' mind. He could not have enough of Shaw, the rebellious incendiary, destroyer of fallacy and fetish: and the theatre might have been a self-appointed Shaw Memorial. Within ten years it put on thirteen of the full-length plays, the entire 'metabiological pentateuch', and even eighteen of the one-acters, often an explosion in a confined space. When GBS died Clunes wrote:[1] 'If I were a painter, I would paint his life in red. I would be thinking of that flaming red beard of the younger Shaw, and of the flaming intensity with which he set light to the rubbish-heap of so many follies and inherited emotional bric-à-brac. The flame is somehow inescapably his emblem—and it persisted until the end.'

Clunes went also to a dramatist on the other bank from Shaw, Arthur Pinero, the farces particularly, though he did unearth such a lost example of the well-made drama as *The Thunderbolt*. (It has since been revived excitingly.) Among the classics he liked Sheridan (five plays) and the Restoration men: Farquhar gave him Sir Harry. There were six major plays by Ibsen, and (a nice variation) six comedies by Maugham, some of them once fashionable and always actable Edwardian legacies. Clunes remembered Granville-Barker and, in two new plays, James Bridie; Masefield and O'Neill, Synge and Sartre. He showed his delight in Chekhov. Without hesitation he pleased himself: the pleasures of an inspiringly catholic actor-manager (in Great Newport Street more manager than actor) whose taste could be registered as much by what he left out as he put in. Not even peevish writers who ignored collectors' pieces and who insisted endlessly on 'something new', could accuse the Arts of neglecting current drama; we find seventeen premières—for repertory a high proportion—among the 132 plays of the first decade. Clunes loved words, their ring and flash and gleam, and as a connoisseur of new writing for the stage he was quick to observe the prose of the young Ustinov and, most notably, the verse of Christopher Fry.

Since the night of May 20, 1942, when he had directed the Odets play with its best of titles, *Awake and Sing,* he, his advisers (Frank Smith never wanting), and his associates had done more for the London theatre than any bleak statistics could suggest. The Arts record reads like a selective history that might have deserved the praise of an O'Casey figure:[2] 'This is a wonderful house, so it is. Afther... standin' in frost, rain, an' snow, frontin' th' winds o'th world, it's a marvel it isn't flat on its face, furnishin' only an odd shelther for a sthray fox, but here it stands...' It was not surprising that, in the summer of 1952, Clunes was dead tired and looking forward to a holiday. 'The effort,' he said, 'has been more than worth-while. Long ago I ceased to expect that we should show any profits. Experience has taught me how, by careful planning, we can continue our work.' In fact, he was approaching the end of his own work at the Arts. There would be another fifteen months, yet already he half-prepared for a freedom he was not resolved yet how to use, probably to indulge in his own form of serendipity, the collection of theatre books. If now and again he withdrew into a private world, it was because he had never believed that actors should be too much together.

When the birthday run of *Hobson's Choice* closed—it had been extended by a week—the Arts slid back about 120 years in stage time to a comic complexity of the 1760s rescued from oblivion (there was a difference of opinion about the need), Arthur Murphy's double intrigue, *The Way to Keep Him.* It was rapidly manoeuvred, especially by Avice Landone, whose description—its least probable line aerated—of a scene at Ranelagh was like a Ruth Draper sketch in miniature; Derek Birch as Lovemore, Garrick's part; Jill Bennett as a maid called Muslin; and Laurence Hardy. Tony Britton, as a minor figure, had a personal distinction. When *The Firstborn* was being cast, his performance as Pharaoh's son had so impressed Clunes, Fernald, and Fry that, ten days after rehearsals began, Clunes had offered him a year's contract; he was the sole contract player on the Arts books.

Pleasant though the Murphy was (several people said Clunes should have acted in it himself), audiences would be better satisfied by John Fernald's rediscovery of a very early Pinero farce, or 'eccentric comedy', *In Chancery:* his last play, it was said, before popularity overtook him, and one unstaged in London since its 1884 première. At Steepleton a commercial traveller (speciality, gas-brackets) loses his memory in a railway crash and finds himself surrounded by women. Reginald Purdell, as the amnesiac, affected a prim, squeezed gravity; Toke Townley, a man on the trail, resembled a sinister steam-kettle; and Valerie Hanson had a mild gentility, as a faint water-colour might have spoken if given the tongue. (It was a play that prompted odd comparisons.)

Clunes came back during September 1952 for *Don Juan in Hell.* He could not keep away from the debate in which Juan, the Statue, the Lady, and the Devil talk their heads off for ninety minutes. Clunes had enriched the voice, the wit, and the style for Shaw's electrical storm in which the lightning quivers about most topics known to man; and David Bird, the very devil of a fellow, produced tones like hot buttered toast. It was a pity there had to be an interval.

Those who so passionately demanded a new play, none of your Shaws and Pineros, nothing 'safe' but, whatever the word might imply, 'relevant'—it was bandied about a lot just then—doubtless had their answer in a sultry American piece, *Two Loves I Have...* Taken by Dorothy and Howard Baker from Dorothy Baker's prizewinning novel, *Trio,* and directed by Roy Rich, it invited such headlines, in the style of 1952, as 'This Sort of Play is Unhealthy', 'For the Shock-Proof', and 'Abnormal Friendship'. It was, as Hope-Wallace put it,[3] 'another gambol in the shade of the Green Bay Tree', dealing efficiently enough with the influence of a lesbian—a distinguished scholar in an American university town—upon a girl student. Some writers praised it for fulfilling a club theatre's duty to treat themes too unconventional for general acceptance. Nobody in those days could impersonate a cobra more persuasively than Sonia Dresdel. Elizabeth Henson was the corrupted girl, looking like Francesca 'all dewy from the convent fetched', and Michael Gwynn was as adept in modern dress as in Stratford Shakespeare. Three West End managements made offers; but it was a long haul to 1968, and—though he had relented over what people called a complementary play, *Third Person*—the Lord Chamberlain refused to license even a modified text. The trouble, we gathered, was that if he agreed it would be hard for him to persist in his ban on a comparable piece, Lillian Hellman's *The Children's Hour,* which still frightened him to death. *Two Loves I Have* had to make do with its brief life at the Arts before it slipped into the dark.

The next play, *Lord Arthur Savile's Crime,* was perfectly innocuous, but a gale blew up because two adaptations of Wilde's story, both with the same title, were announced within a fortnight. Alec Clunes was angry. The Royal Court management, quite unabashed, said compacently: 'The publicity will be helpful to the Arts and ourselves.' Clunes did not agree; and the Court dramatist was annoyed because his script, which he had submitted to the Arts in May, had come back three weeks later. The argument rattled on, and so eventually did the plays. The Arts production, a fortnight after its rival, was the luckier; Stephen Murray directed it like a pastrycook whipping the cream, and Walter Hudd's butler ruled the night, pouring the poison with a more discreet dignity than anyone in or out of Belgrave Square. Yet, if the story had to be dramatised, one would have expected Wilde to have done it himself over sixty years before. Possibly it was a warning that he did not.

A negligible English version of Jean Cocteau's *Les Monstres Sacrés* (as *The Holy Terrors*) owed everything to the virtuosity of Fay Compton. Happily, Christmas lay ahead, and with it Clunes' return to his favourite *Maria Marten* (by 'a well-connected author'): everything lavishly guyed, a lot of not always apposite balladry, a gipsy's warning, a rooftop chase, and the cast acting with joyful desperation. Sonia Williams, grabbing like an alert scrum-half, snatched the baby from before a clanking locomotive that slid, majestically and sinuously, round its stage track: one of Clunes' Sensational Spectacles. He was as apt with fires as with locomotives, and his cottage blaze was a pretty bit of arson in a holiday humour. We cannot wonder that *Maria* broke Arts records for the previous decade, and that the next piece had to be postponed to allow her to go on running.

So many managements jostled for position in 1953, Coronation year, that by midsummer the theatre list was too crowded for comfort. The Arts moved along calmly with a programme that might have represented, in microcosm, the whole of its last eleven years: one (disastrous) new play, otherwise a soundly-ordered list that took in Maugham (twice), Shaw (naturally), Bridie, Chekhov, and Strindberg. Maugham's *The Breadwinner*, a New Year gift of a comedy the Arts already knew, gave way to Strindberg and the agonising tragedy of *The Father*, directed tautly by Peter Cotes and memorable for the reappearance in London, after a long provincial exile, of the incalculable Wilfrid Lawson. When inspired, a condition nobody ever prophesied, he could burn through the night like a blow-torch: this is what he did as the finally strait-jacketed Captain. Though the precise quality of the livid piece must be arguable, its husband and wife (Beatrix Lehmann here was steel and ice) belong to the Theatre, Theatrical at its meridian; Lawson, knowing what to do in the grand manner, deserved his welcome home. Cautiously, Clunes, who had not forgotten a misguided Mark Antony in an Old Vic *Antony and Cleopatra* twenty years before, had arranged to see that Lawson did not drink too much; his care was justified but elaborate planning worked, and the notices were as good as any in the actor's career, few of the important epithets neglected.

Next John Fernald had to cope with two plays quite alarmingly different. The Arts had long relied upon him, as a director, to speak with Chekhov's voice. Now he offered an unflawed production of *The Seagull* that held all October in its eyes and was aided by such performances, without parade of any kind, as Michael Gwynn's Konstantin and the Trigorin of Alan MacNaughtan. Good; but over the next piece Fernald, professional though he was, must have presided with mounting horror. Entitled *Second Best Bed,* it was by N. Richard Nash, an American dramatist who might have been running a high fever when he contemplated the personal life of Shakespeare, a subject treated in dialogue that had what Gilbert's Lady Jane would have called 'a tender bloom like cold gravy'. Those who recalled Nash's adroitly-contrived school tale, *The Young and Fair* could not understand how anyone who wrote so sensitively then could have handled Shakespeare so crudely. Alan MacNaughtan never lost heart. The audience did.

It was a comfort to get back to the Arts mascot, Bernard Shaw (who had certainly known about a stage Shakespeare in *The Dark Lady of the Sonnets*). *Arms and the Man,* after sixty years, was warmly alive. Clunes (he had not had a score of parts in all his arduous years of management) played Bluntschli for the first time, and directed: a farewell to the writer he praised above all others. Mild, gently, quizzically-smiling, and in easy command, he was Shaw's man, needing only a little more voice. With him he had Robin Bailey, who could strike a good sugar-stick attitude as the romantic exhibitionist, Sergius Saranoff (last acted in the West End by Olivier), and Gwen Cherrell as the purring girl Raina, fed upon Byron, Pushkin, and the opera seasons at Bucharest. It could be only a small anti-climax to partner this with Wolf Mankowitz's brief Jewish fantasy, *The Bespoke Overcoat,* Alfie Bass as a kindly ghost who returns to get an overcoat from the man who had 'sweated' him to death.

These were cheerful days at the Arts even if, in common with so many London theatres, it suffered from a hustle of late-comers. Unpunctuality had been a West End vice, not simply at premières. The Arts tried to cope tactfully by inserting in late-comers' programmes (except those on first nights when nobody could guarantee the time of starting) a sketch by Ronald Searle, headed 'Gentle Hints Department', of two arrogant late arrivals fighting their way to their seats. Whether it helped much is doubtful; but it was a useful notion, and collectors were glad of Searle's drawing. The device was employed first at performances of *Tobias and the Angel,* Bridie's most endearing comedy.

So, swiftly, to the end of the season and to Clunes' goodbye to the Arts. After *Arms and the Man* he had effectively left Great Newport Street: tired, he proclaimed, of working eight hours a day as an executive and acting at night (though these matters seldom coincided). Anyway, he was anxious to re-charge his energy and to concentrate for a while (but not too long) upon his book-collecting and his new bookshop. That was the story; yet, totally unpredictable, he was engaged in a long West End part, the title-role of *Carrington, V.C.* at the Westminster, when the lease of the Arts—which for more than eleven years had occupied so much of his energy and pleasure—was sold for £19,000 during November 1953. At first it had been thought that the buyers would belong to a consortium headed by Hugh Hunt; but eventually, after William Wordsworth had acted as mediator, they were outbid by another experienced theatre-man, Campbell Williams.

1   In *Theatrical Companion to Shaw,* ed. Raymond Mander and Joe
     Mitchenson (Rockliff, 1954), p. 301.
2   Sean O'Casey: *Purple Dust,* Act 2.
3   *Time and Tide,* 11.10.1952.

CHAPTER EIGHT
POST-CLUNES: 1954–1956

Campbell Williams, previously managing director of the theatre ticket agency, Keith Prowse, sustained some of the now established Arts tradition, with his wife as co-director. There had to be changes: a far larger proportion of new plays, nearly seventy between the end of 1953 and the beginning of 1962; hardly any (three or four at most) of the late-Victorian and Edwardian revivals that so gratified Alec Clunes; and many plays of foreign derivation, French, American, Italian, Spanish, but especially French. John Fernald continued his artistic direction until he was appointed Principal of the Royal Academy of Dramatic Art in 1955, and Roy Rich also lingered for a while until he moved back into films. During the 1950s the most important change in direction was the arrival of the young Peter Hall, fresh from a score of University productions at Cambridge; at the Arts, where he remained for eighteen months, he began his professional career.

The year 1954 opened with Gaston Baty's distillation of *Crime and Punishment* for which Fernald based his treatment upon Baty's own: a patchwork of brief scenes, carefully composed and lit. For all Fernald's assiduity and his players' response, the piece appeared sometimes to be a wry comment on the darker Russian drama. Yet, whenever we began to doubt, it did take charge of the mind, and its Sonia (Rosalind Boxall) conveyed the girl's submissiveness without weakening to a washed-out sketch. That agreed, the Arts was happier, on the whole, with Charles Hawtrey's *The Private Secretary,* a choice (allegedly from the German) that Clunes would have approved, for he insisted that genuine culture had room in it for farce. Here it had room for the funereally timid Reverend Robert Spalding, pale young curate of Victorian routine, with his goods and chattels (goloshes, bath-bun, 'acidulated drop') and the complicated slap-bang through a country-house: not much more than a catch-as-catch-can skirmish, though we were laughing in 1954 at many of the things that had convulsed 1884. Harold Goodwin, rejecting the comic-curate bleat, pounced on Spalding's true worried gravity, a tooth-and-nail resolve to make himself understood among environing terrors.

He, his chattels, and his desperation yielded to Lorca's Spanish melodrama, *Blood Wedding,* tale of a blood feud, seizure of a bride from a bridegroom, passionate love, a forest flight, lamentation and death: a plunge into the romantic-tragical sometimes oddly translated. Peter Hall, in his first Arts play, used his strong pictorial sense to get Lorca across, the semi-lyrical passages, the evocation of a moonlit wood of contorted trees. Beatrix Lehmann added her intensity. Even so, the play remained intractable; it had been better as a ballet.

Giraudoux's *The Enchanted,* under Fernald, did a lot to atone. The joy of the fantasy, moonshine with a philosophical core, is that anything can happen to its people, a phantom by a lake, a romantic Inspector of Weights and Measures, and the marvellously bewildered Mayor of a small French town. More and more, too, could happen at the Arts. The theatre pressed on resourcefully to Goldoni and Pirandello, coming to a pause (among general delight) at the home of Charles Pooter (George Benson), The Laurels, Brickfield Terrace, London, N., during 1888: every character possible from the Grossmiths' *The Diary of a Nobody,* assembled under the precise direction of Basil Dean. With Richard Blake he had compiled 'six chapters for the stage'. An enduring book, it seemed likely to be just as durable in the theatre; but Gowing and Cummings, Murray Posh, Burwin-Fosselton and the rest could have no West End theatre until the following June when their life was brief. The cast, meanwhile, had been much altered.

There would be an earlier transference (though five months elapsed) for Fernald's revival of *Saint Joan.* He had the fortune to direct Siobhan McKenna, the Irish actress, as the girl Shaw called 'the most notable warrior saint in the Christian calendar and the queerest fish among the eccentric worthies of the Middle Ages': a phrase that had angered many as GBS knew it would. Siobhan McKenna grew in performance; opening less like the pillar of faith and fire that is Joan than an Irish Peter Pan or a lass of Lorraine (via Galway). But in the trial and epilogue she was the tormented Joan who could reach that 'terrible anger' of the stage direction, filling the imagination where, previously, she had teased it. During the epilogue she entered wearing (in place of full Joan armour) a red gown, dress of the Irish peasant girl in whose tones she spoke. After thirty years the play was still what some of the prescient had said it was on a spring night in 1924, an unflinching modern classic; from the Arts it went for a few weeks to the St. Martin's.

That autumn Peter Hall reappeared, now as director of *The Immoralist,* Ruth and Augustus Goetz's free (and, one hazarded, cheapened) version of Andre Gide's novel. At its close audiences were aware that only the emotional power of Yvonne Mitchell and Michael Gough were preserving interest in a luckless marriage and a tedious text. It could have been fuel for George du Maurier's old drawing of a pair of spectators during a French season in London, captioned: 'We go to see the acting; we do not wish to understand the play.'

Half-a-dozen productions in 1955 had special reasons for remembrance. John Whiting came back to the theatre of *Saint's Day* with his version of *Une fille pour du vent* (the sacrifice of Iphigenia at Aulis), a title which does point André Obey's meaning more sharply than the English *Sacrifice to the Wind*. The theme is stated dramatically; midway, arguments for and against the sacrifice are too protracted. The play is not long; directed by Stephen Murray, it was done at the Arts without a break, Helena Hughes persuasively the girl who goes out to die. There was a curious choice of curtain-raiser, Eugene Ionesco's exercise in the crazy-macabre, *The Lesson*.

There had been no more detailed and elaborate work at the theatre for a long time than Peter Hall's production of Julien Green's *South*. The piece begins on Sunday, April 11, 1861, in the South Carolina house of Bonaventure; elsewhere, at twenty minutes past four in the early dawn of April 12, 1861—the exact moment when the curtain falls—a white haired Virginian farmer, 67 years of age, fires the first Confederate cannon-ball towards Fort Sumter, and the American Civil War has begun. We imagined that Green, having chosen such a period, would be dramatising life in a chosen (and fictional) plantation household during those hours when North and South drew breath before the fight. Certainly he dramatised it, but it was hardly the play we could have wished for in the circumstances. Once he had created the right kind of intense atmosphere, he diverted our minds from the issues of the war to others of more limited interest. Hall was anxious to assert that, though the Lord Chamberlain had refused a licence for public performance, *South* was 'not primarily about homosexuality; this was only a thread in Green's tapestry'. In performance we were worried by the dramatist's refusal to explain himself; the amorous criss-cross appeared to be a small matter compared with the fury about to break over North America. Still, we had to respect Denholm Elliot's clenched quietness, his response to what a critic called the 'doomed love' of an abnormal young Polish officer; André Morell's banked-up misery as the plantation-owner; Zena Walker's impressionable 17-year-old; Lyndon Brook, as he carried off an unlikely last scene; and Clare Austin's final tragic cry over the body of the man she loved. *South* reached the Arts in the dead vast and middle of a newspaper strike; in consequence, it was under-publicised; and it had to linger in shadow until, some years later, there was a less expert performance at the Lyric, Hammersmith.

Peter Hall had succeeded to the full artistic direction of the theatre. John Fernald, over the years the most versatile and controlled of men, staged his last production before leaving for a decade at RADA:

another French play for a theatre that, from the earliest years, had upheld *l'entente cordiale*. *The Midnight Family*, translated from Charles Dorat by Gillian Winter, began with an uncanny first act in a Montmartre flat; the second, after lapsing into maladroit prose-poetics, developed into an adventure in the macabre, an example of French dramatists' preoccupation with death. The writing was uncertain; but Fernald as usual never dulled device by coldness and delay; he was fortified by Emrys James, the feyness of Elaine Wodson, and Rosalind Boxall's matter-of-course humanity.

Nobody, so far as we know, charged the young Peter Hall with lack of endeavour. In June 1955 he put on in the bandbox of the Arts (sets by Paul Mayo) Eugene O'Neill's *Mourning Becomes Electra*, a feat that might have satisfied some directors for a season. In this four-and-a-half hours' endurance test we are, uncomfortably, in the grip of the Mannons, a family that stands for the House of Atreus in a New England scene. For any audience the trouble is O'Neill's resolve to say nothing once if he can say it three times. At the Arts all rested (as so often) on the playing, ruled by Mary Morris, whose Lavinia resembled a cistern of coiled snakes, and with Mary Ellis, Joseph O'Conor, Ronald Lewis, and (as the murdered general) John Phillips, ready throughout to transcend the material.

There followed a work which, *Saint's Day* aside, would be as contentious as any in Arts record: *Waiting for Godot* (*En Attendant Godot*). The piece is a metaphor for what, in a tiresome period cliché, is known as 'the human condition'. To-day, when Samuel Beckett's fantasy and its stream-of-consciousness tramps, sitting by the roadside, is so familiar, it is difficult to hark back to August 3, 1955, when most of the audience, as baffled as the actors had been in rehearsal, waited for light to break upon their darkness. We might say now tht *Godot* is 'poor in the essence of happiness—rich only in never-ending unrest. In it there meets a combination of antithetical elements at eternal war. Driven hither by objective influences, wafted one moment into blazing day by mocking hope, plunged the next into the Cimmerian darkness of tangible despair, it is but a living ganglion of irreconcilable antagonisms'. A good and portentous summary, though the words are from another context, those of Ralph Rackstraw in *HMS Pinafore*. 'I hope I make myself clear, lady,' he adds; whereupon Josephine replies: 'Perfectly. (*Aside:*) His simple eloquence goes to my heart.' Gilbert might have enjoyed *Godot*. Peter Hall directed it cunningly, and the piece was acted with the most unflurried zest by Hugh Burden ('This is getting really insignificant') and Peter Woodthorpe in the double act of the tramps; Timothy Bateson, a chalk-faced, hopelessly dejected broken clown of a slave, who had the cascade-delivery of a sub-Joycean monologue; and Peter

Bull as a well-nourished bully of mounting blood pressure, the slave-driving Pozzo.

Just before *Godot* opened a fashionable West End life at the Criterion, Peter Hall had directed at the Arts another uncommon piece, an Italian dramatist Ugo Betti's *The Burnt Flower-Bed,* set by a frontier, 'the point of attrition between two huge wheels', and translated by the poet Henry Reed. On the theme of responsibility and prickling with symbolism, the drama lived in its impressive cast: Yvonne Mitchell as a wife in a daze of sorrow, Alexander Knox as a man trapped, Leo McKern as a dangerous political schemer, and Esme Percy as a politician terrifed and broken. It is obvious that in those days there was little room for the mayfly-comedy. The year 1955 kept thoroughly determined: few frivolities, but few grumbles from a membership that had stuck by the Arts through every variation and would not defect.

Only two more plays that year. The first, *Komuso,* had created a haunting atmosphere on sound-radio; some at the première expected this to be repeated. It could hardly be so, for on radio the stage directions were spoken, and the Arts script, doing without them, used lengths of dialogue that sounded prolix. Robert Nichols, the author, had been a regarded Georgian poet. The play, found after his death among his papers at Cambridge, was established in an ancient Buddhist temple, high above a Treaty port in southern Japan, and founded on a phrase, 'No one can have too much compassion', spoken by a lost, sad idealist (Michael Warre). An often elusive anecdote, it was still in some ways an experience.

Christmas soon afterwards produced neither a re-jigged melodrama nor a resolute farce. Instead, there was a new children's play, probably, if it is to be lasting, as awkward as anything to write. Only a very few have run through the years. It did look as if the Arts might have got something permanent in *Listen to the Wind* (by Angela Ainley Jeans; music and lyrics by Vivian Ellis) about children kidnapped by gypsies, and their friends flown down from the Kingdom of the Winds to rescue them. Somehow it was not instantly revivable; its hour can return. Peter Hall and his cast—Miriam Karlin as a mermaid—were in ebullient spirits; and Nora Nicholson, who played a fantastic grandmother, recalled it all affectionately in her autobiography[1] years ahead: 'Having completely lost my singing voice, I was allowed to speak my numbers to the music.' (Nobody minded.) Everything was brisker than the first production of 1956, *Darkling Child,* where a girl from Bedfordshire in the 1660s, caught in a maze of emotional and religious 'possession', was arrested beside the coffin for the murder of her father. Not exhilarating, but by sheer concentrated strength a new actress, Margaret Whiting—later to be an Old Vic Cleopatra—forced the play on our attention.

In February, as a highly dramatic farewell to the Arts, Peter Hall directed *The Waltz of the Toreadors* by Jean Anouilh, most prolific dramatist of his period, so prolific and temporarily so influential that Allardyce Nicoll, major historian of the stage, used 'From Aeschylus to Anouilh' as the second title of a definitive work, *World Theatre.*

The latest piece (*La Valse des Toréadors* had been acted four years earlier in Paris) was once more about bitterness, the evanescence of love; its note might have been the Chekhovian stage direction,[2] 'Marsh-fires appear'. It introduced again the General from *Ardèle* and his wife, the woman who had screamed (off) like a peacock, and who now (on-stage) was readier to dance: a grim skeleton-dance that halted the laughter. Translated by Lucienne Hill, its broad, sour, smoky comedy, and its sudden throat-catching rasp as if one were taking quinine, with Strindberg's approving ghost standing by, made of it at the Arts, and later at the Criterion (700 performances) something to be heard, seen and tasted. Directed with great aplomb by Peter Hall, and acted relentlessly by Hugh Griffith as the General who had rogued and ranged in his time, and (in her single scene) by Beatrix Lehmann, this could have reminded some of the lines, 'The dead are dancing with the dead, the dust is whirling with the dust'.

It was talked of more than its successor at the Arts, a musical version (score almost inevitably by Julian Slade) of *The Comedy of Errors* from Shakespeare's salad days. The librettists, if this is right for Lionel Harris, who also directed, and Robert McNab, confined most of the lyrics to a single word, or phrase ('Quoth I, quoth he'), or added such borrowings as 'Should he upbraid', 'I shall no more to sea', 'A cup of wine', and, neatest, 'When you have vowed', which is a snatch from *Measure for Measure.* The cast guided us agreeably through the tangle of mixed identities, 'sweethearting' (as Julian Charles Young's coachman said of *Othello*), and wholesale recognition. There were few grumbles (members were glad to laugh again without irony), and there would have been fewer still if everyone had recalled what Frederick Reynolds did to the play at Covent Garden in 1819—'When icicles hang by the wall', from *Love's Labour's Lost,* sung against a backdrop of snow-covered mountains. But *The Comedy of Errors* has usually been more or less fair game as we have observed from various Stratford-upon-Avon revivals.

1   *Chameleon's Dish* (Elek, 1973), p. 125.
2   *The Seagull*, Act 1.

CHAPTER NINE
MATTERS ARISING: 1956–1958

This was a period in the London theatre for which an epigraph could have been 'Insurrection, with one accord, banded itself and woke'. It woke on the night of May 8, 1956 when younger people, who, it seemed, had been chafing under their wrongs, found a cheer-leader. He was John Osborne, an actor-dramatist; his play, *Look Back In Anger,* put on by the English Stage Company, a new 'writers' theatre' at the Royal Court in Sloane Square, was a surge of fluent invective. Not much of a play, it did say what rebels wished to hear, and its call from the next room (a phrase from Whiting's *Saint's Day*) set off at once a blast against contemporary life in general; a demand for 'social realism' and the kind of relishingly outspoken piece now given an imprimatur. Besides challenging the commercial stage, this touched even the club theatres. Self-consciously at first, the Arts would cease to move across the accepted repertory in the manner Clunes had initiated. Now a free-lance actor at Stratford and elsewhere, the policy in Great Newport Street undeniably puzzled him.

During the early summer of 1956 Robert Shaw wrote *On the Mainland,* a more or less psychological melodrama, an island story, violent in action, lukewarm in recollection; he acted a principal part himself. Sally Benson's American *The Young and Beautiful* began as if it were a clinical study of a girl with a passion for dramatising herself, and ended in something like tragedy. A revival of *The Children's Hour* was yet another club theatre attempt (after those at the Gate and the New Boltons) to deal—theoretically in private—with Lillian Hellman's banned Lesbian narrative: in it a girl, as evil as Iago, wrecks the lives of her two schoolmistresses. The Lord Chamberlain continued to keep aloof.

Peter Hall had left the Arts. When he resigned in July 1956 Peter Wood, aged 29 and most recently director at Oxford Playhouse, succeeded him (and staged four of the plays between November 1956 and January 1958). He opened with an Ionesco double bill, *The Bald Prima Donna*—a nonsense-title—and *The New Tenant.* In the first of these Eugene Ionesco, master of the cliché, conducted a mad symposium, an hour of inconsequential ribbon-building, in the suburban drawing-room of a Mr. and Mrs. Smith. 'Goodness gracious! How very amazing!' said Jill Bennett over and over, like a cracked gramophone record. *The New Tenant* was just as odd: a sly, secret faun of a man (acted inimitably by Robert Eddison) all but buried alive beneath a preposterous, cumulatively growing mound of eccentric furniture. If we refused to let a chain of non-sequiturs exasperate us, it was a wholly comic evening—and, after all, that was probably Ionesco's idea.

For Christmas this caprice was followed by the least obscure of melodramas, a production (Walter Hudd's) that would certainly have gone well at an earlier Arts. Tom Taylor's *The Ticket-of-Leave Man* (1863) lives for its famous moments in the tavern:

> HAWKSHAW (*pulls off his rough cap and whiskers and speaks in his own voice*): Hawkshaw, the detective. (*Gives a pistol*). Take this—I'll be on the look-out!

The old piece reached the Arts as stoutly-carpentered sensation-drama, prodigal in detail and with plenty of implicit social criticism, though little to excite the Theatre of Protest. For nine-tenths of the evening Hudd resisted any temptation to fool the text, a change for audiences that had been told Victorian drama was huge fun. Most of them left with admiration for the playing of John Trevor (hero) and George Coulouris (Hawkshaw, the detective), as well as with a certain respect for Tom Taylor. Goodness gracious! How very amazing!

Very little mattered during 1957: Armand Salacrou's mediocre comedy, *No Laughing Matter* (no tactful title) which Alec McCowen, Brenda Bruce and Paul Daneman fortified as best they could; Mervyn Peake's *The Wit to Woo*, its blank-verse profusion maybe better on the page than the stage; and a totally misconceived production of Genet's *The Balcony*. But, in effect, the theatre had to wait until November for a night of authentic excitement, the quick flame of *The Public Prosecutor*. Surprisingly, Fritz Hochwälder's French Revolution drama (no response from the Royal Court) never went to the West End. Kitty Black had translated it; Alan Badel directed, and played the leading part; and 'the office of the French Republic in the prison of the Conciergerie' resembled a segment of a lion's cage. This indeed was what it was—though we know that Carlyle preferred to call the dangerous lion Fouquier-Tinville 'ferret-visaged'. It was as a trapped lion that Alan Badel prowled across the stage on the last day of the Terror in August 1794, the deadly Prosecutor failing to realise until the twelfth hour that he had been caught. It was absorbing to watch this confident intriguer pinned, helpless, while the judge and witnesses he had chosen brought him to doom in the silent, gloating presence of Theresia Tallien, 'Madonna of the Revolution'.

After Christmas, on the whole a good time for it, the Arts offered a curiosity—it could be nothing else—that, years before, Clunes might have appreciated: a fantasy, suggested by Sheridan le Fanu's 'Green Tea', in which a small black monkey haunts a mid-Victorian clergyman with a past. Lilian and Edward Percy, in what they re-titled *A Stranger in the Tea*, had sought to build a substantial stage play round this anecdote of a soul's disintegration. An honourable failure, it did allow Robert Eddison to suggest the aspen-trembling fear of the man with a tortured mind.

The theatre had known its Eugene O'Neill from the compactness of *Anna Christie* to the endurance of *Mourning Becomes Electra*. Now, in *The Iceman Cometh*, Peter Wood's final production, at the end of January 1958, the stage became through four-and-a-half hours a rooming-house run by Harry Hope (significant name) in the New York of 1912, 'a cheap ginmill of the five-cent whisky, last-resort variety; situated on the downtown West Side'. Or, in another definition, uttered by the sardonic Larry, 'the No Chance Saloon... Bedrock Bar'. For an audience this must always be a lost land, the hiding-place of those pathetic backroom boys in the ebb of their journey. They linger in a pocket of the imagination much as they are when the night opens: shadows waking slowly to join the blundering charade that returns them finally to death-in-life. 'No one,' says a spokesman, 'had to worry about where they are going because there is no further that they can go. It's a great relief to them.'

The intimacy of the Arts helped, for the players were thrust upon us as upon each other. We saw them roused reluctantly at the summons of Hickey, a travelling salesman, who proved to be the biggest pipe-dreamer of the lot and the most tragic. Some of us did wish that O'Neill had pruned the verbiage of his fourth act, Hickey's confession before the policeman led him off into the dark. Yet here Ian Bannen's anguished glibness was as right as the response of his fellow-derelicts, together (in Kipling's phrase) 'for things we never mentioned, for art misunderstood'. We did not wonder when the play was taken to the Winter Garden, though equally we understood why, on that immense stage (one the Arts had not forgotten), the *Iceman*, like much else, drooped and died.

CHAPTER TEN
MARKING TIME: 1958–1961

After O'Neill the Arts was too often marking time: it escaped infrequently from work that could be little more than well-meaning. Ronald Duncan's conversation for three, *The Catalyst*, concerned a doctor who would have been happy in a polygamous community; his wife, and his mistress. *Quiet Honour*, almost a footnote to the Wolfenden Report, considered homosexuality in public schools. *Templeton*, by Anthony Lock, was a three hours' sprawl of political melodrama; and in Gabriel Marcel's *Ariadne* we appeared to be treading a labyrinth with no real hope of finding the centre.

Without warning, then, we had a night's call to attention, welcome because critics had been treating the Arts with perilous languor (thus: 'It was surprising that one member of the cast wore the same pair of socks for thirteen years, and in three continents'). Everyone woke up for a double bill by Tennessee Williams, *Garden District*, collective title for two plays, one long, one short, that had nothing in common except their setting, the wealthiest district of New Orleans, and their dramatist's horrific imagination: that of a dramatist who, in the mood, would get on both his own nerves and ours. Though he could over-write feverishly, he could also conjure a devil's brew of atmospherics as in the longer play, *Suddenly Last Summer*, which ended after the description of a man's death, torn to pieces by a cannibal-crowd of starving children. Agreed, it was a narrative professionally told; our revulsion was mixed with admiration, and there could be little argument about the performances of Patricia Neal as a girl (on the verge of entering the State Asylum) with a tormented scream, and of Beatrix Lehmann as a relentless old crone, a twisted red spider. It puzzled many listeners that *Something Unspoken* (which came first) had been licensed for public production; but acted as it was by Beatrix Lehmann and Beryl Measor as employer and employed, baffled cat and watchful mouse, it could undeniably hold the stage.

Productions less stern included (now in a redecorated theatre) an Anouilh double bill translated by John Whiting and—another Arts return—directed by Peter Hall, only a year away from his appointment to Stratford-upon-Avon. The better piece, and the more substantial, *Traveller Without Luggage (Le Voyageur sans Bagages)* dealt in the dramatist's familiar fashion with memory and identity before it slackened, at the last, into the comic-fantastic. Kenneth Jupp had written *The Buskers,* splendidly directed by Toby Robertson, about a troupe of what, in far South Cornwall, used to be called expressively 'pomping folk', established in 'a field on the edge of a wood in Europe'. Reluctantly, the members of an odd family, passionate, subtle, brutal, or senile, sought to present on a stage within a stage what had happened ten years ago, so that they might discover its meaning. There was some promise among its multiplying echoes (Pirandello seemed to have been an influence), and Patricia Jessel and June Brown helped to make the night worth-while. As for the American *Ulysses in Nighttown* where the dramatist Marjorie Barkentin had tried to chart a passage through Joyce's phantasmagoria of Bloom and Daedalus, chaos among Circean visions from a Dublin day, this was probably an attempt at the unattainable. Burgess Meredith directed, and the theatre had never had to cope with so large a cast: seventy-one parts, any amount of quadrupling, quintupling, and more. Zero Mostel, who had acted in London only at the Palladium, came over to repeat his New York Bloom: a protean player (with shining boot-button eyes) of striking alertness and plasticity. But it had to be every spectator for himself.

Little else lingers from 1959. Presently Eugene O'Neill, seldom long absent from an Arts programme, reappeared in the spring of 1960 with *A Moon for the Misbegotten.* Coping in his own determined style with a physical freak of a Connecticut farm girl ('twenty-eight... five foot eleven in her stockings, and able to do the manual labour of two ordinary men'), he ran on about her and about the guilt-haunted alcoholic going maudlin in the moonlight. An intermittently tiresome affair, it owed much to Margaret Whiting who, by an effort of creative imagination, got us to credit the woman both at first and when— according to a stage direction—she changed to her 'Sunday best' and we saw her as 'a gentler, sadder being'.

Discussion of this would wane before the arguments over Harold Pinter's *The Caretaker* which Donald McWhinnie directed, with Donald Pleasence in a subtle portrait of low cunning; Alan Bates, and Peter Woodthorpe. Pinter was still not taken seriously. *The Birthday Party* had no particular impact, and *The Caretaker,* a spectacular improvement, would be the first full-length piece in which most people acknowledged his bizarre talents. About survival and loneliness, it was the tale of two strange brothers, a cluttered room in a West London suburb, and a tramp who could never get to Sidcup (what he would do if he got there was his own problem). One of the brothers observed—and it might have been Pinter on his own method—'I take nothing you say at face value; every word you speak is open to any number of interpretations.'

Today the play is so familiar that it is hard to revive any early antagonism to it and to a highly skilled production. Soon transferred to the Duchess, it assured its author's name in the London theatre.

That was the only Arts transference of 1960, and we could not be surprised. An Ionesco double bill (a new departure for the highly individual Richard Briers) might have been visualised when the dramatist was doing gymnastics. After *The Caretaker* the best of the year's plays was *Naked Island,* an Australian, Russell Braddon's picture of life in the notorious Changi gaol at Singapore during the last summer of the war. Braddon had known Changi from the inside; his memories, in a set designed by Ronald Searle, himself a former prisoner, reached us as the sharpest truth, the record of one group, mainly Australian, and of its tensions, friendships, and character-development during captivity. The occasion was heightened by the performance of John Neville, the classical actor from the Old Vic—later a director in Canada—as a man whose quiet exterior hid profound emotion.

Naked Island, in the autumn, was a change, for the Arts had a habit at the time of doing its most likely plays early in the year. But 1961 opened moderately with a triple bill, called simply *Three:* one choice first-rate, a second hovering on the edge, a third disappointing. John Mortimer's *Lunch Hour,* funny and moving, about an over-anxious business man and an office girl at an assignation in a dingy railway-district hotel, had Emlyn Williams as the man who realised in a brand of hazy despair that his own caution had betrayed him, and Wendy Craig as the girl who misused a precious break. The single-minded N.F. Simpson's *The Form* was a game of inconsequences in which, seeking to express the sheer lunacy just beneath the surface of life, he worked out his joke too soon. Emlyn Williams—here gallantly siphoning speeches through his moustache—was also in the third play, a Pinter misfire entitled *A Slight Ache.* The bill was welcomed politely enough to go on to a short run at the Criterion.

The rest of the year had nothing comparable: it covered a portentous business—serious, or so we hazarded—about free love in Africa, as well as a quite superfluous version of *Lady Chatterley's Lover.* Playgoers, still ready to stand by the Arts, moved towards 1962 without noticeable zest.

CHAPTER ELEVEN
EXPERIMENTAL WING: 1962–1963

Some quick changes now: Peter Hall who had become director of the Royal Shakespeare Theatre at Stratford-upon-Avon, and a man who had known everything about the Arts, back and front, arranged for the theatre to be leased temporarily as an experimental wing of the RSC. This had already a London base at the Aldwych; the Arts, in support, could concern itself with roughly the type of play that, allowing for variations in taste, would be staged twenty years on at the Warehouse studio in Seven Dials, or at The Pit in the new Barbican. During February critics went to Great Newport Street more expectantly than for some time.

The first RSC production opened on March 13: *Everything in the Garden* by an experienced writer, Giles Cooper. Nobody during the years had led us so fiercely up the garden path; we had no idea that what seemed to be a fragile satirical comedy would turn to a bitter outburst against hypocrisy, expediency, and greed. An early scene might have been the beginning of a comment on suburban gentility, less sour than in the Royal Court vein and treated with finesse by Derek Godfrey (any husband proud of his garden) and Geraldine McEwan as his wide-eyed, sparrow-chirping wife. Slowly, sourness grew. The girl had advertised for a job; a *procureuse* arrived to offer lucrative afternoon work in Wimpole Street. When money was discovered all over the place, when the husband had duly erupted, and when a conventional cocktail party had assembled, we still imagined (at the première) that the dramatist had contemplated a mildly satirical joke. But in mid-party the Madam appeared; all the wives were revealed as her 'girls'. She must leave Wimpole Street and open a house in the suburbs, so why not there at Woodfield Green? Immediately everyone was involved; greed flourished. The little comedy had loomed into a thundercloud-morality; the tea-kettle was a boiling cauldron, and Cooper kept it boiling to the end. With a cast partly changed, the play had a brief run at the Duke of York's.

Midway through the Arts life of *Everything in the Garden* the theatre merged quietly into the New Arts. On March 15 Nat Cohen had bought the outstanding eleven years' lease for £30,000, and the changed name was used on programmes for the RSC's second and less acclaimed production, *Nil Carborundum* by Henry Livings. As 'experimental' as a Whitehall farce of the period, this was merely an exuberant and formless document of peace-time in the RAF, with a few shrewd incidental observations; it ended in the chaos of a night 'exercise' that defied coherence. Doubtless, in the old days, Alec Clunes, with his refusal to forget the classics, would have agreed with the move from this to Toby Robertson's revival of *The Lower Depths,* Gorki's Russian dosshouse at the turn of the century. Sombre and uncompromising with a certain midnight beauty, it was something wider audiences should have shared. One player towered: Wilfrid Lawson as Luka, the wanderer, who is gentle because he has been through the mill so often. Sfiff, stocky, his slow voice convulsively exact, he dominated the night by force of imagination.

A fourth RSC play introduced David Rudkin, a writer who would be recognised in the future, but who was seldom so provocative as in *Afore Night Come.* During its first hour 'in an orchard in a rural pocket on the crust of the Black Country', we might have assumed that Rudkin, a Black Country man himself, was trying to write a statement of life in the pear orchards somewhere near Bromsgrove, a useful tape-recording of the drearier forms of idiomatic speech, interlaced by offstage banter shouted from tree to tree. Towards the end of the second hour somebody said: 'I reckon things have got a bit out of hand.' They had. Once the interval had passed it was afternoon, a thunderstorm was threatening, a farcical orchard-owner whipped to and fro with an equally farcical daughter at his heels, a woman picker fell from a tree offstage, and it grew plain that some of the yokels thought of a new and voluble casual labourer from Limerick as an Irish Jonah. Black clouds piled, knives were honed, light and symbolism thickened. We guessed there might be ritual murder too grim for the eye, and about a quarter of an hour before the end three of the illiterate workers despatched the old Irishman, beheaded him, and removed him for tarpaulin-wrapped burial in the orchard depths. Such good players as Paul Dawkins, Roger Croucher, Peter McEnery and Timothy West helped loyally to people the orchard; but the one fine thing in a night that occasionally generated horrific power was Clifford Williams' taut, watchful production, his manipulation of passages that could have been on the razor-edge of parody. The play was revived at the Aldwych in 1964.

These performances had been valuable for the RSC, though Peter Hall was reminding us that a major undertaking could not afford to live on its Press notices: money seemed to be flowing down the Thames faster than it came in. Still, the RSC continued with its versatile New Arts choices: the fifth of them Thomas Middleton's Jacobean *Women Beware Women,* with the sinister high comedy of its famous chess game,

Plate 13. Rediscovering Chekhov: John Fernald's production of Chekhov's rarely-played *Ivanov* (April 1950). Left to right: Richard Warner (Borkin), Michael Hordern (Ivanov), Hugh Pryse (Count Shabelsky) and Helen Shingler (Anna Petrovna). (*Photograph: Houston Rogers; Collection of Mrs. Clunes*)

Plate 14 (above). Fighting the fire at the Arts Theatre in August 1951 — an impression in oils painted by Michael Warre on the spot. Thanks to tremendous efforts by the actors and theatre staff, the production of C.E. Webber's *Right Side Up* had to be deferred by only four days.
(Photograph: Michael Kerr; Collection of Michael Warre)

Plate 15 (below). Alec Clunes in one of his favourite parts — Don Juan in Shaw's *Don Juan in Hell.* This revival in September 1952 shows also Gwen Cherrell as Doña Aña, David Bird as the Devil and Richard Warner as The Statue.
(Photograph: Angus McBean)

Plate 16. Frank Barrie in his one-man show, *Macready!* given at the Arts in September 1981.

and an insight into feminine psychology that had not been studied in the theatre for three centuries. Some hit-or-miss performances did not help the tortuous plot, but two players were applauded as definitive. One was Pauline Jameson as Livia, personification of intrigue ('O, the deadly menace that women set for women,' Middleton says); and the other, Ernest Milton as the Cardinal, a small part for an old master: he had what Kent saw in the face of Lear, authority. Many would remember the sight of his ascetic features and the sound, among the clouding incense, of that grave, hypnotically mannered voice as it uttered Middleton's final moral—above a stage as heaped with dead as that in the ebb of *The Spanish Tragedy.*

Only two further RSC plays remained, of which the first and infinitely more telling, Boris Vian's *The Empire Builders* (done in Paris during 1959 as *Le Bâtisseurs d'Empire*) set most writers guessing wildly. The scene was a grim house beyond which we heard intermittently a skirling and shrieking as of tropical birds of prey; at each warning the family climbed to an upper floor, always smaller, progressively cheerless. At length there was a single survivor. In an attic lit by a single window the father tried to rationalise his situation in a long monologue that ended in death, noise, darkness, and the stage filling momentarily with faceless corpse-figures. Some assumed that Vian was considering man's increasing loneliness at the approach of death; but it appears that, with this and other theories, we should all have borne in mind Alfred Jarry's 'Pataphysics is the science of imaginary solutions'. Simon Watson Taylor, who translated the piece admirably, said: 'All things being equal, I will call it a passionate hoax, a supremely non-avant-garde anti-symbolist play that allows everyone to form his own opinion, with no help from the author (but plenty of clues leading up false trails)...' That said, we had more than once the sense of a dramatist creating more powerfully than he knew. David Jones, the director, provided an apparatus of nightmare; and Hugh Burden and Lally Bowers, as husband and wife, were thoroughly in the spirit. So was Freda Dowie as a maidservant who talked like a page from a thesaurus. A weird yet haunting occasion, far more so than the RSC's last play, *Infanticide in the House of Fred Ginger* (by Fred Watson) of which only the title stays, as well it might.

We expected it to be quiet at the New Arts when the RSC had gone. Yet three or four plays of some merit took us to the end of the year and through the beginning of 1963. In the autumn of 1962 the novelist Muriel Spark's first comedy, *Doctors of Philosophy,* was described in the redecorated theatre's programme (and in words a little dulled by use) as an opening bid 'to establish the Arts Theatre Club as a key centre of the arts, and to fill a gap in the London cultural and social scene': something, we imagined, that had always been the idea. *Doctors of Philosophy,* directed by Donald McWhinnie, and led by Gwen Cherrell, Laurence Hardy, and Fenella Fielding, had a witty first act in a highly academic household near the Regent's Canal, a second fuzzed like a foggy negative, and a third that restored some of the early vigour. Later, in *A Cheap Bunch of Nice Flowers,* not perhaps a compulsively attractive label, another novelist, Edna O'Brien, added modestly to theatrical memories: her Dublin narrative of the relationship between a doomed mother and a girl beset by fantasy could be forcible, and one doubted whether, in the context, the acting of Eithne Dunne, Susannah York, and Marie Kean (maidservant) could have been improved.

Neither of these plays has survived in the repertory; but James Saunders' *Next Time I'll Sing to You* (January 1963) has done so: an unpredictable result. He is a hill-and-valley writer, and this early conversation piece for five players at a rehearsal, 'suggested by a theme' from Raleigh Trevelyan's book, *A Hermit Disclosed,* seemed to some listeners (grateful for the acting of Michael Caine and Michael Bryant) simply a desolation of debate, with the dramatist self-consciously aware. 'If there was a point,' says one of the characters, 'all this would be beside it.' Agreed; but we could see later—though not at the Arts—what Saunders could do when he rose from the valley to a work of such strong imagination as *A Scent of Flowers* (Duke of York's, 1964).

Later, during the spring of 1963, the Arts introduced to the English stage the South African dramatist, Athol Fugard. *The Blood Knot* of the title was a bond between brothers—a Negro and a white man, born of the same mother but of different fathers, and living in a shack at a 'coloured' location near Port Elizabeth. The brothers' attitude in a tormented (but sometimes affecting) dialogue represented the behaviour of two races living side by side. The play could repeat itself crudely, but performances of mingled sincerity and technical address by the South African Zaiken Mokaes and the English Ian Bannen helped to give theatrical form to a plot at that hour surprising.

Selectively, we can take two other plays from the year. Anybody who left Elizabeth Hart's version of E.M. Forster's novel *Where Angels Fear to Tread,* after the first act, would have despaired too soon. Having begun halfway through the book, the dramatist had to dispose of a thick layer-cake of exposition: a poor preface to a narrative that, once it had got to Italy, retained respect. English visitors were urging a young Italian father to surrender a four-months-old son; tragedy supervened. Glen Byam Shaw directed quickly on a revolving stage; Michael Denison had depth and repose as a man who said, 'I am fated to pass through the world without moving it or colliding with it'; and Keith Baxter (the Italian) did not allow the showiness of the part to affect his judgment, as it could well have done. The production was transferred profitably to the St. Martin's.

Finally, a double bill by Harold Pinter lived on its first play, *The Lover*, technically assured in its tale of a married couple's attempt, by erotic masquerade, to revive the early fires of their marriage. A theatrically less skilful partner, *The Dwarfs* (which began on radio), depended upon a garrulous young man (John Hurt) who uttered long swathes about a covey of imaginary, garbage-picking dwarfs: hardly the richest company for half a night.

CHAPTER TWELVE
FOR ALL AGES: 1964–1981

Over a decade the theatre's reputation had waned; but on paper its list for the first seven months of 1964 looked sound; Marlowe (in fact the *Edward II* revival from Leicester was insensitively noisy) and Ibsen as classical dramatists; Frank Marcus, Joe Orton, and Alan Ayckbourn as new ones; and the most kindling one-woman performance the Arts had staged, *The Brontës* by Margaret Webster; formerly an Old Vic actress and, in New York, an eminently sane Shakespearian director, she was a gifted woman fitted to her group portrait of an extraordinary family— the three sisters of Haworth, from childhood in that bleak parsonage to the moment in 1861 when, every flame extinguished, the household furniture was sold; the mahogany table where the sisters wrote, the sofa on which Emily died. Unflinchingly emotional, it had to be presented as it was on that foggy January night; to be spoken as Margaret Webster spoke Emily's 'Cold in the earth', or Charlotte's letters. Throughout, we never lost the sense of genius in isolation.

The next première revealed the most persuasive Hedda Gabler since Jean Forbes-Robertson's on the same stage. There is no compulsory blue-print for such a part as this; Joan Greenwood reminded us of a lynx in cut-glass, her languid, frigid voice matched to the strange creature, possessive, frustrated, and a mocker; she did not falter at the third-act burning of the manuscript, a scene that had foxed too many Heddas. Minos Volanakis directed in the Max Faber version which always (and the phrase is by no means obvious) made sense.

This year had a third success: a comedy by Frank Marcus, who would be acknowledged soon as drama critic and dramatist. In its fashion *The Formation Dancers* was like a contemporary *Private Lives:* theatrical glitter about four people, a pompous literary parasite; his wife, who was Everywoman; his best friend, a self-deluding playboy; and his friend's mistress, as much a child of nature (though of a different race) as Aloma of the South Seas during the mid-twenties. The play did not pretend to be more than an amusing caper; the most serious figure—and she would never be able to express the reason—was the girl of the period, called Perdita and acted smoulderingly by Joanna Dunham. With Robin Bailey, Maxine Audley, and Gerald Flood comparably truthful, transference to the Globe was certain.

This was infinitely more agreeable than *Entertaining Mr. Sloane,* a first play by Joe Orton, also sent to a West End run, just round the corner at Wyndham's. Orton would become a fashionable dramatist, discussed hyperbolically before and after his sudden death. For some his work would be an acquired taste. Not everybody at the Arts could applaud his black comedy from a house in the middle of a rubbish-dump; many found its characters (testy old man, arch middle-aged daughter, husky young tough) as repellent as the working-out of the plot. It was acted, however, with loyal spirit, and it would certainly have a future, not only in the theatre but also during debates on an unanswerable question: what constitutes a sense of humour? During the autumn of 1965 one obvious production for the records—but by no means obvious at the time—was the much gentler *Mr. Whatnot* by a young man named Alan Ayckbourn. Only the manager, Peter Bridge, who had seen it at the Victoria Theatre, Stoke-on-Trent, had judged from a mild trifle the prolific and inventive writer to be, strengthened by his talent for choosing a presumably insoluble stage problem and solving it, unfussed. Few people backed Bridge's perception. At the Arts, where it reached us as a country-house comedy in disguise, told mostly in mime, with appropriate sound effects and back-projection, *Mr. Whatnot* was all rather like the brush of a mayfly's wing. Its life was a little longer than a mayfly's. Ayckbourn has not revived it.

By now the average Arts play slipped by, hardly noticed in a vague progress. Work for children, put on in growing profusion by Caryl Jenner and Matyelok Gibbs of the Unicorn Theatre, was usually the most acceptable. We could go seldom to such a revival as a *Man and Superman* (November 1965), later at the Vaudeville. Alan Badel exercised his velvety, springing voice as Tanner, and Sian Phillips was a reasonably good Ann. It seemed right, in one sense, that it should begin at the Arts where Clunes, who so relished the Don Juan interlude, had never been able (owing to a Shavian caprice in old age) to do the full play. But ironically, though the familiar framework was there, the 1965 *Man and Superman* failed to take us to Juan's 'Void near Hell'.

The New Arts had been governed at first by Nat Cohen (chairman), Norman Matheson, Kenneth Rive (managing director), Peter Hall, Sir Fordham Flower (of Stratford-upon-Avon) and David Deutsch; Michael Codron as managing director. During the spring of 1966 the theatre reverted, wisely, to its former name, the Arts without prefix, and with a new Board: Alfred Esdaile (chairman), Peter Birtwistle (managing director), John Reynard, Barry McDonald, and Sir Fordham Flower. Just before these took over there had been 'a comic biography', Roger Milner's *How's the World Treating You?,* re-written since a Hampstead trial and with a pleasant grave idiocy ('When we first married we had a little flat in Leicester; we didn't want to be too near the centre of London'). Not much happened otherwise. *The Three Musketeers,* treated as a chaotic rough-and-tumble, was as tedious as this kind of thing usually is. Conversely, an adaptation of *Pride and Prejudice* was suitably decorous and authentic; if its acting, in general, had had the manner of Petra Davies' Elizabeth and Joan Haythorne's Matterhorn of Lady Catherine de Bourgh, the night might have been conspicuous. We remember, too, a performance in a different mood, the return of Pinero's too often neglected *The Thunderbolt,* aided by the emotional truth of Peggy Thorpe-Bates and Brian Oulton.

Soon the Arts underwent further and more drastic change. From 1967 titles with a splash of fantasy had begun to fill the programme: *The Royal Astrologers, The Prince, the Wolf, and the Firebird, The Tingalary Bird, The Lord of the Amber Mountain.* Playgoers of between four and twelve had trooped in during the afternoons for the kind of direct imaginative invention that their age-groups had scarcely known. The change was due to a most sympathetic and experienced theatre-woman, Caryl Jenner (the pseudonym of Pamela Penelope Ripman) who since 1962 had used the Arts at Christmas to stage new children's plays. Previously her English Theatre for Children (and its various touring companies) had flourished; and it was this that leased the Arts in 1967 as the Unicorn Company, the first all-round young people's theatre in Britain. Caryl Jenner directed most of its work herself, with Matyelok Gibbs and Ursula Jones. The Unicorn Theatre booked evening productions as well. Though (as the Appendix shows) they represented a catholic taste, not many really counted. Still, there was such a matter as a triple bill (under Caryl Jenner) in February 1968: *The Farce of Death Who Almost Died* by Michel Ghelderode, Chekhov's *The Proposal,* and—a wistful backward look to the earlier Arts—Shaw's 'startling, original, pathetic, blood-curdling, and entrancing' tragedy, *Passion, Poison and Petrification; or, The Fatal Gazogene.* That June an almost forgotten, and dangerously fumbling, piece by Galsworthy, *The Foundations,* was revived. Malcolm Taylor, in 1971, treated with his sharp intelligence Dylan Thomas's *Under Milk Wood,* already a contemporary classic.

When Caryl Jenner died in 1973, at the age of 53, Matyelok Gibbs succeeded her as artistic director, and Ursula Jones as resident director. Until 1977 the Unicorn lease was confined to the theatre itself, but it took over then from Peter Birtwistle, on a 21-year lease, the entire Arts building. Nicholas Barter, who became artistic director, had had adult experience at Ipswich and Lincoln, and with the RSCs touring Theatregoround.

Two evening plays ran so long about this time, *Kennedy's Children* (1975) and Tom Stoppard's *Dirty Linen* (from 1976) that people who had been getting accustomed to the Arts as primarily the headquarters of the Unicorn Theatre for Children, began again to think of it as adult. *Kennedy's Children,* an intelligently imagined American piece, done originally on the Fringe, at the King's Head in Islington, lasted for a year. Its successor, *Dirty Linen* (1976–1980) was an amiably uninhibited free-for-all about a House of Commons Committee; fairly minor work for Stoppard, it took immediate possession and was still at the Arts, after many cast changes, well over three years later. From a medley of occasional short runs since then, the only event we need to mention here is the one-man show, *Macready!* (1981) in which Frank Barrie restored one of the most misunderstood actors of the nineteenth century. The 'deeply and inexplicably moving' William Charles Macready (of whom Tennyson wrote in a farewell apostrophe, 'Thine is it that our Drama did not die!') bequeathed to the stage the memories of his generosity, his angers, his formality, his shyness, his loyalty, his egotism, and his undeniable greatness. Frank Barrie, who animated him with the richest understanding, performed this programme across the world. (We have often wondered what Macready and Clunes might have had to say to each other; at some points there could have been an intuitive respect.)

EPILOGUE

Alec Clunes, who died aged 57, on March 13, 1970, must endure as the man who restored the Arts when it seemed to have slid into oblivion. During his lifetime what his friend Norman Marshall would call the 'other theatres' of London (known by a cluster of names, studio, club, fringe, experimental) had always lived dangerously. Some, as various as the Everyman and the Gate, and afterwards the Boltons, the Lindsey, and the Torch disappeared. At Swiss Cottage the Embassy was re-born as a school of acting. Fresh names arrived, notably Hampstead Theatre Club which James Roose-Evans established as early as 1959; and, in later years, mainly post-Clunes, an efflorescence of such public-house stages as the King's Head, Islington, and the Bush. But the Arts, especially, did for more than a decade the task that no other theatre had attempted; it looked after the English repertory, bringing back play upon play that hardly anybody—we do not forget Bernard Miles' Mermaid—has since deigned to revive. It took, as we have seen, much from the Shavian canon, including the minnows (a pleasant bonus for collectors, if glum financially). It was also, in Clunes' time, the first home of such contemporary excitements, far differently received, as Fry's *The Lady's Not For Burning* and Whiting's *Saint's Day;* and it sustained numerous expert performances. After Clunes, when among a battalion of directors were John Fernald, Roy Rich, Peter Hall, David Jones, Donald McWhinnie, it could serve in its fashion as a microcosm of the day's stage (*Waiting for Godot, The Waltz of the Toreadors, The Caretaker*). Certainly, in the mid-20th century (this book's principal term) its place is secure.

First of all, we have to remember Alec Clunes: for his convictions and his resolve to keep them; for his presence, his sense of period, his warm, flexible baritone. More anxious as a rule to direct than to act, something of a dictator, unremittingly a perfectionist, he found it hard to deal with anybody he could not respect; the Arts, its people and its plays, moved in his beliefs. If he had once fixed upon a course, he would seldom vary it; he realised what the Arts ought to do, and he held to this.

From his beginning in London he had never lost the idea of a theatre of his own; it was a high day for him when he impressed such persons as Peter Elstob and Beecher Moore (a wealthy American whose father had originated various modern methods of accounting) with his plan to revive—but with neither a public licence nor public money—a derelict club in Great Newport Street. He and his advisers, especially Frank Smith who had known him from his youth but who kept in the background, gave to the Arts new life and living. Alec (never on the Board) chose his plays, through eleven years, in the context of stage history; he appeared himself less than his admirers wished, but when he did, as Sir Harry Wildair ('Egad, this burgundy makes me speak like an angel'), or Don Juan ('Hell is the home of the unreal and the seekers for happiness'), or Moses ('There is a wilderness between my blood and peace'), we could know the dimensions of great playing. In so many ways it had to be a sad hour for the theatre and himself when, on a drive home from the Edinburgh Festival of 1953, with a batch of new scripts in the back seat, he decided in a country by-lane that his task in Great Newport Street was over. True, he was far more successful in his own right than he could have expected when, twenty years before as a soldier in the Old Vic *Antony and Cleopatra*, he had to remember to come from the steps on his left foot at the seventh beat of the drum. If he wished, he could be at home anywhere in the theatre at large. Yet the Arts had been his own creation, and without it his professional world had to be curiously incomplete.

He was married, most happily, to Daphne Acott. He became progressively concerned with his bookshop, his writing (*The British Theatre,* 1964), his life on the perimeter. Illness overtook him; he died during the spring of 1970. Bernard Shaw, next to Shakespeare, was his favourite dramatist, one he had served with unwavering fidelity. It could be said of him in the Shavian words for a writer:[1] 'He who has nothing to assert has no style and can have none; he who has something to assert will go as far in power of style as its momentousness and his conviction will carry him.' Remembering Alec Clunes with gratitude, we know how far he went.

1   Preface to *Man and Superman.*

APPENDIX I
PLAYS PRODUCED AT THE ARTS THEATRE CLUB
(Professional productions only;
also omitting programmes of ballet, dance and mime)
Names of Directors included where available

1927

20 April:	*Picnic,* a revue by Herbert Farjeon (Dir. Harold Scott)
6 May:	*The Lady of Belmont,* by St. John Ervine (Dir. Milton Rosmer)
31 May:	*The Bridge,* by Kate O'Brien (Dir. George Owen)
5 July:	*Nevertheless---,* by Silvia Blennerhassett (Dir. Gertrude Kingston)
17 July:	*Samson and Delilah,* by Sven Lange (Dir. Michael Orme)
14 September:	*Master,* by Marjorie Ling (Dir. Cedric Hardwicke)
23 September:	*Scrapped,* by Alma Brosnan, revised by Miles Malleson (Dir. Henry Oscar)
2 October:	*The Duchess of Elba,* by Rudolf Lothar and Oscar Ritter-Winterstein, English version by Avery Hopwood (Dir. Nigel Playfair)
15 October:	*Frenzied Finance,* By Noël Shannon
27 October:	*Where the Cross is Made,* by Eugene O'Neill *Woman's Honour,* by Susan Glaspell
30 October:	*Yolande and Sylvain,* by Newton Ferrers (Dir. Michael Orme)
6 November:	*The Peaceful Thief,* by Audrey Lucas (Dir. Molly Kerr)
10 November:	*Blind Man's Bluff,* adapted from the French of Charles Hellen and Pol D'Estoe *Collusion,* by George Middleton *Save the Mark,* adapted from the French of Nancy and Manoussy by "Pharamond" (Dir. Henry Oscar)
20 November:	*The Glimpse of Reality,* by Bernard Shaw *Creditors,* by August Strindberg, translated by Edwin Bjorkman

27 November:	*For First-Class Passengers Only*, by Osbert and Sacheverell Sitwell (Dir. Gertrude Kingston)
3 December:	*Nathaniel Bendersnap*, by George Dunning Gribble (Dir. Cyril Wood)
14 December:	*La Prisonnière*, by Edouard Bourdet, English version by Gilbert Wakefield (Dir. Maurice Browne)
29 December:	*Tod, the Tailor*, by W. Griffin

1928

28 January:	*Lithuania*, by Rupert Brooke *The Fascinating Foundling*, by Bernard Shaw *Simoon*, by August Strindberg *The Land of Heart's Desire*, by W.B. Yeats (Dir. Henry Oscar)
4 March:	*Flies and Treacle*, by C. Dudley Ward
25 March:	*The Way*, by Constance Malleson (Dir. Charles Carson)
1 April:	*The Making of an Immortal*, by George Moore (Dir. Robert Atkins)
5 May:	*For Better, for Worse*, by May Edginton (Dir. Reginald Denham)
11 May:	*Let's All Talk About Gerald*, by A.A. Milne (Dir. Norman Loring)
17 June:	*Prejudice*, by Mercedes de Acosta (Dir. Leslie Banks)
1 July:	*The Tragic Muse*, adapted by Hubert Griffith from the novel by Henry James (Dir. Athene Seyler)
15 July:	*Down Wind*, by C. Dudley Ward
26 July:	*Thunder on the Left*, adapted by Richard Pryse from the novel by Christopher Morley (Dir. Harcourt Williams)
12 September:	*Payment*, by C.E. Openshaw (Dir. E. Lyall Swete)
4 October:	*The Pocket Money Husband*, by John Gliddon
10 October:	*Easter*, by August Strindberg (Dir. Allan Wade)
17 October:	*The Fountain Head*, by Ashley Dukes (Dir. Beatrice Wilson)
25 October:	*The Workhouse Ward*, by Lady Gregory *Birthright*, by T.C. Murray *The Shadow of the Glen*, by J.M. Synge (Dir. William G. Fay)

30 October:	*The Power of Darkness*, by Leo Tolstoy, English version, Mr. and Mrs. Aylmer Maude
	(Dir. Michael Orme)
2 November:	*The Fruits of Enlightenment*, by Leo Tolstoy, English version, Mr. and Mrs. Aylmer Maude
	(Dir. W. Keith Moss)
21 November:	*Caravan*, by Max Möhr (Dir. Cecil Lewis)
29 November:	*The Clandestine Marriage*, by George Colman and David Garrick (Dir. Auriol Lee)
9 December:	*The Lion Tamer*, by Alfred Savoir
	(Dir. Nicholas Hannen)
28 December:	*Wallflower*, by Audrey Scott
	(Dirs. Harold Scott and Elliott Seabrooke)

1929

5 January:	*The Lady With a Lamp*, by Reginald Berkeley
	(Dirs. Leslie Banks and Edith Evans)
23 January:	*The Age of Unreason*, by Zak Bryn, adapted from the Norwegian by G.M. Gathorne-Hardy
	(Dir. George Owen)
30 January:	*Full Moon*, by Emlyn Williams (Dir. John Fernald)
9 February:	*Black Velvet*, by Willard Robertson
	(Dir. Franklin Dyall)
24 February:	*The Prince Consort*, by Reginald Berkeley
	The Likes of 'Er, by Charles McEvoy
	(Dir. Esme Percy)
20 March:	*The Tidings Brought to Mary*, by Paul Claudel, English version by Louise Morgan Sill
5 April:	*The Theatre of Life*, by Nicholas Evreinof and Fernand Nozière; adapted by George Paston
	(Dir. Frank Birch)
12 April:	*The Infinite Shoeblack*, by Norman Macowan
	(Dir. Leslie Banks and the Author)
25 April:	*Captain Banner*, by "George Preedy" (Marjorie Bowen)
26 May:	*Johannisfeuer*, by Hermann Sudermann, performed in German (Dir. Michael Orme)
1 June:	*Sybarites*, by H. Dennis Bradley
	(Dir. Athole Stewart)
22 June:	*Heels of Pleasure*, by the Ranee of Sarawak
	(Dir. Margaret Yarde)
27 June:	*Red Sunday*, by Hubert Griffith (Dir. Komisarjevsky)

3 July:	*Young Love,* by Samson Raphaelson
	(Dir. George Zucco)
13 July:	*The Hell Within,* by Guido Stacchini
	(Dir. Norman Macdermott)
21 July:	*These Pretty Things,* by Gertrude Jennings
	(Dir. Nicholas Hannen)
24 July:	*Gentlemen of the Jury,* by Francis A. Compton
	(Dir. John V. Trevor)
27 July:	*The Speyg,* by A.D. George (Dir. Franklin Dyall)
18 September:	*Veronica,* by C.K. Munro (Dir. Allan Wade)
25 September:	*Miss Julie,* by August Strindberg
	Pariah, by August Strindberg
	(Dir. Michael Sherbrooke)
2 October:	*Time and the Hour,* by Douglas Murray
	(Dir. Henry Oscar)
8 October:	*Improper People,* by Rodney Ackland
	(Dir. Aubrey Mather)
16 October:	*Dancing Shadows,* by John Protheroe, adapted from
	Marcel Pagnol's *Jazz* (Dir. Allan Wade)
1 November:	*Through a Window,* by Andrew Richardson
	(Dir. Reginald Bach)
13 November:	*Chinese White,* by Val Gielgud
	(Dir. Owen Nares)
24 November:	*La Prisonnière,* by Edouard Bourdet, performed in
	French (Dir. Alice Gachet)
1 December:	*Wills and Ways,* by Halcott Glover
8 December:	*Shadows of Strife,* by John Davison
	(Dir. H.K. Ayliff)
10 December:	*People Like Us,* by Frank Vosper

1930

5 January:	*The Humours of the Court,* by Robert Bridges
	(Dir. Brewster Morgan)
12 January:	*The Devil,* by Benn W. Levy (Dir. The Author)
22 January:	*Nine Till Six,* by Aimée and Philip Stuart
	(Dir. Auriol Lee)
26 January:	*Aimer,* by Paul Geraldy, performed in French
29 January:	*On the Quota,* by Halcott Glover
	(Dir. Michael Sherbrooke)
5 February:	*The Command to Love,* by Rudolf Lothar and Fritz
	Gottwald, adapted by Herman Berstein and Brian
	Marlow; revised for the English stage by Bernard
	Merivale (Dir. W. Graham Browne)

16 February:	*Das Blaue von Himmel*, by Hans Chlumberg, performed in German
2 March:	*Phèdre*, by Racine, performed in French (Dir. Alice Gachet)
16 March:	*La Piccola*, by Massimo Bontempelli, performed in Italian (Dir. Viola Tree)
20 March:	*A Doll's House*, by Henrik Ibsen (Dir. Henry Oscar)
30 March:	*After All*, by John van Druten (Dir. Auriol Lee)
8 April:	*It's a Pity About Humanity*, by Miles Mander (Dirs. Oliver Baldwin and John Hastings Turner)
13 April:	*The Man With the Portfolio*, by Alexei Fairo, performed in Russian (Dir. Komisarjevsky)
30 April:	*Jitta's Atonement*, by Siegfried Trebitsch; translated by Bernard Shaw (Dir. Henry Oscar)
15 May:	*The Ugly Duchess*, adapted by Vera Beringer from the novel by Lion Feuchtwanger (Dir. W.G. Fay)
22 June:	*Faust*, Part One, by Goethe, performed in German
25 June:	*Jealousy*, by Louis Verneuil; English version by Eugene Walter (Dir. Auriol Lee)
2 July:	*The Procurator of Judea*, by Anatole France; adapted by Patrick Hamilton *S.S. Tenacity*, by Charles Vildrac (Dir. Clare Eames)
8 July:	*The Macropulos Secret*, by Karel Capek (Dir. A.R. Whatmore)
16 July:	*The Devil and the Lady*, by Alfred Tennyson *The Dumb Wife of Cheapside*, by Ashley Dukes (Dir. Nigel Playfair)
23 July:	*Dance With No Music*, by Rodney Ackland (Dir. Auriol Lee)
17 September:	*Monsieur Brotonneau*, adapted by Ruth Chatterton from the French of Robert de Fleurs and G.A. de Caillavet (Dir. George de Warfaz)
28 September:	*Devant La Porte*, by Henri Duvernois *La Voix Humaine*, by Jean Cocteau *L'Occasion*, by Jacques Normand and Georges Rivollet; all in French (Dir. Alice Gachet)
15 October:	*Little Eyolf*, by Henrik Ibsen (Dir. Michael Orme)
22 October:	*Mr. Eno, His Birth, Death, and Life*, by C.K. Munro
6 November:	*Machines*, by Reginald Berkeley (Dir. Henry Oscar)

23 November:	*Sturm im Wasserglas,* by Bruno Frank, performed in German (Dir. Michael Orme)

1931

14 January:	*The Velvet Mask,* by Maurice Rostand, translated by Norman Stuart (Dir. Beatrice Wilson)
22 January:	*The Circle of Chalk,* revised version by James Laver after Klabund (Dir. Matthew Forsyth)
4 February:	*Who Goes Next?* by Reginald Simpson and James Wedgwood Drawbell (Dir. Frank Gregory)
12 February:	*"If",* by Lord Dunsany (Dir. Robert Atkins)
1 March:	*Lui,* by Alfred Savoir, performed in French
4 March:	*O.H.M.S.,* by Reginald Berkeley (Dir. Athole Stewart)
17 March:	*Hedda Gabler,* by Henrik Ibsen
15 April:	*Tomorrow,* by C.B. Fernald (Dir. John Fernald)
22 April:	*The Years Between,* by Edward Poor Montgomery (Dir. Peter Godfrey)
6 May:	*Make Up Your Mind,* by Leopold Marchand, adapted by Xenia Lowinsky (Dir. Henry Oscar)
13 May:	*The Mantle,* by Basil Mason (Dir. Robert Atkins)
29 May:	*The Trial of Jeanne D'Arc,* by Edward Garnett (Dir. Henry Oscar)
1 July:	*Demos, King and Slave,* by Henri Ghéon; English translation by Barry Jackson; verses translated by John Drinkwater
27 September:	*Behold the Bridegroom,* by George Kelly
8 October:	*Vile Bodies,* by Evelyn Waugh (Dir. Nigel Playfair)
4 November:	*Othello,* by William Shakespeare (Dir. Michael Orme)
15 November:	*Musical Chairs,* by Ronald Mackenzie (Dir. Komisarjevsky)
25 November:	*Passing Through Lorraine,* by Lionel Hale (Dir. John Fernald)

1932

3 January:	*1066 and All That,* adapted by Michael Watts from the book by W.C. Sellar and R.J. Yeatman (Dir. Esmé Church)
20 January:	*The Judgement of Dr. Johnson,* by G.K. Chesterton *The Comforter,* by Laurence Housman (Dir. Norman Macowan)
27 January:	*Avalanche,* by Beverley Nichols (Dir. Esmé Percy)

8 March:	*Captain Desmond, V.C.*, by Maud Diver
	(Dir. Howard Leslie)
16 March:	*Rudolph of Austria*, by Graham Rawson
3 April:	*Pelléas et Mélisande*, by Maurice Maeterlinck, performed in French
13 April:	*Bewitched*, by Clive Currie (Dir. Walter Brodie)
24 April:	*The Mews*, by Theodore de Serannes
	(Dir. Esmé Church)
12 June:	*At It Was In The Beginning*, by Merton Hodge
	(Dir. John Fernald)
28 September:	*Many Women*, by Florida Pier (Dir. Esmé Percy)
9 October:	*Spacetime Inn*, by Lionel Britton
	(Dir. Reginald Bach)
26 October:	*The Gates of Ur*, by W.G. Hole (Dir. Evan John)
6 November:	*Other People's Lives*, by A.A. Milne
27 November:	*All's Well That Ends Well*, by William Shakespeare
	(Dir. Robert Atkins)
14 December:	*Silver Wedding*, by Ruby M. Ayres
	(Dir. Reginald Bach)

1933

8 January:	*In Vino Veritas*, by Walter Hudd
	The Long Christmas Dinner, by Thornton Wilder
	Suppressed Desires, by Susan Glaspell
	(Dir. John Fernald)
11 January:	*Things That Are Caesar's*, by Paul Vincent Carroll
	(Dir. Lennox Robinson)
22 January:	*Lady Audley's Secret*, by C.H. Hazlewood
	Count Albany, by Donald Carswell
	(Dir. Tyrone Guthrie)
26 January:	*The Comedy of Good and Evil*, by Richard Hughes
5 February:	*These Two*, by Lionel Hale (Dir. John Fernald)
13 February:	*Mademoiselle Julie*, by August Strindberg; French translation by Charles de Cazanove
	(Dir. Georges Pitoëff)
16 February:	*La Ronde*, by Athur Schnitzler; French translation by Suzanne Clauser, M. Remon, and W. Bauer
	(Dir. Georges Pitoëff)
22 February:	*Maison de Poupée*, by Henrik Ibsen; French translation by M. Prozor (Dir. Georges Pitoëff)
24 February:	*Joë et Cie*, by Hjalmar Bergman; French translation by Lissi Olsson (Dir. Georges Pitoëff)

1 March:	*The Lake*, by Dorothy Massingham in conjunction with Murray Macdonald (Dir. Tyrone Guthrie)
10 March:	*La Souris*, by Edouard Pailleron, performed in French
15 March:	*Cecilia*, by Allan Monkhouse
	The Grand Cham's Diamond, by Allan Monkhouse (Dir. Henry Oscar)
21 March:	*The Lonely Road*, by Michael Orme (Dir. The Author)
26 March:	*Ghosts*, by Henrik Ibsen (Dir. Malcolm Morley)
29 March:	*Bellairs*, by Halcott Glover (Dir. Robert Atkins)
23 April:	*Hamlet* (First Quarto) by William Shakespeare (Dir. Ben Greet)
27 April:	*For Better, For Worse*, by Louie Waddington
	Growing Pains, by Louie Waddington
14 May:	*The Sowers*, by Jean Giono, translated by Jolliffe Metcalfe (Dir. Esmé Percy)

1934

4 March:	*A Doll's House*, by Henrik Ibsen, translated by William Archer
29 April:	*Secret Orchard*, by Claude Roger-Marx and John Leslie Frith (Dir. Stephen Thomas)
6 May:	*The Lawyer and the Roses*, by Jerzy Szaniawski; English version by Ruth Collins Allen (Dirs. Malcolm Morley and Ida Teather)
13 May:	*The Springtime of Others*, by Jean-Jacques Bernard; English translation by John Leslie Frith (Dir. Irene Hentschel)
27 May:	*Viceroy Sarah*, by Norman Ginsbury (Dir. Tyrone Guthrie)
24 June:	*Colonel Wotherspoon*, by James Bridie (Dir. H.K. Ayliff)
30 June:	*La Prisonnière*, by Edouard Bourdet; English version by Gilbert Wakefield (Dir. Maurice Browne)
16 September:	*Five in Amsterdam*, by Ian Rankine (Dir. Muriel Pratt)
7 October:	*No Greater Crime*, by J.A. Jerome (Dir. Ben Welden)
4 November:	*Quartet*, by Cedric Wallis (Dir. George More O'Ferrall)
18 November:	*Take Heed*, by Leslie Reade (Dir. Harold Mortlake)
2 December:	*Glory Be*, by Arnold Ridley

| 30 December: | *'Tis Pity She's a Whore*, by John Ford |
| | (Dir. Gibson-Cowan) |

1935

27 January:	*The Copy*, by Helge Krog, translated by Roy Campbell
	Miss Julie, by August Strindberg, translated by Edward Bjorkman
17 February:	*Mated*, by Christopher Sandeman and Gerald Wynne Rushton (Dir. Fred O'Donovan)
14 March:	*Swords for Utopia*, by Anthony Bertram (Dir. George More O'Ferrall)
24 March:	*Short Circuit*, by Alec Coppel (Dir. Fred O'Donovan)
7 April:	*Basalik*, Peter Garland
15 April:	*Many Mansions*, by Lechmere Worrall
28 April:	*Echo*, by Fletcher Allen (Dir. Fred O'Donovan)
1 May:	*Great Cats Play Chess*, by George Graveley (Dir. Charles Hudleston)
30 May:	*Rossetti*, by Herbert de Hamel and R.L. Mégroz
6 June:	*Broomstick*, by Bonner Semple Dunkerson (Dir. Oskar Ebelsbacher)
16 June:	*The Benefit of the Doubt*, by Arthur Wing Pinero
21 June:	*Pigs in Glory*, by Erwin Pahr (Dir. Esmé Percy)
30 June:	*Love of Women*, by Aimée and Philip Stuart (Dir. Margaret Webster)
23 July:	*The Mysterious Universe*, by Aubrey Menon, based on the book by Sir James Jeans. Music and lyrics by Peter Mendoza and Reginald Bristow (Dir. The Author)
28 July:	*Green of the Spring*, by Muriel Sheehan-Dare (Dir. The Author)
13 September:	*The Harlot*, by Alfred W. Paxton (Dir. John Lloyd)
22 September:	*The Philanthropist*, by Cyril Campion
24 September:	*Dusty Ermine*, by Neil Grant
2 October:	*The Second Key*, by Mrs. Belloc Lowndes (Dir. Reginald Tate)
6 October:	*Pirate Mallory*, by Mary Pakington (Dir. Fred O'Donovan)
18 October:	*Cul de Sac*, by Elsa Malik (Dir. The Author)
29 October:	*Hide and Seek*, by Bymme Warth
3 November:	*Wholly Matrimony*, by Christopher Sandeman and Gerald Wynne Rushton (Dir. Fred O'Donovan)

13 November:	*Kingdom Come*, produced anonymously; presented by Cosmic Comedy
29 November:	*The Future That Was*, by Francis Deverell (Dir. John Lloyd)
15 December:	*Sail Away*, by Stephen Vagliano (Dir. Kim Peacock)

1936

5 January:	*Repayment*, by John Beanes and Evan John (Dir. Evan John)
12 January:	*Luck of the Devil*, by Ladislaus Fodor; English version and lyrics by Lynton Hudson. Music by Michael Sayer (Dir. Leonard Sachs)
26 January:	*Glory*, by Francis Stuart (Dir. Fred O'Donovan)
9 February:	*L'Heure du Berger*, by Edouard Bourdet (Dir. Gerald M. Cooper)
16 February:	*Bright Star*, by Dorothy Hewlett (Dir. Leonard Sachs)
21 February:	*After October*, by Rodney Ackland (Dir. A.R. Whatmore)
1 March:	*Cold Comfort Farm*, by Mabel Constanduros from the book by Stella Gibbons (Dir. Dennis Arundell)
15 March:	*Ehen Werden Im Himmel Geschlossen*, by Walter Hasenclever, performed in German
19 April:	*Indian Summer*, by Aimée and Philip Stuart (Dir. Dennis Arundell)
9 May:	*Little Ol' Boy*, by Albert Bein (Dir. Muriel Pratt)
19 May:	*Too Famous for Words*, by Stein Bugge, translated from the Norwegian by M.B. Hill in collaboration with the author who directed
24 May:	*An Apple a Day*, by Ralph Timberlake (Dir. Andrew Leigh)
7 June:	*When the Bough Breaks*, by Henrietta Leslie and Laurier Lister (Dir. Murray Macdonald)
14 June:	*Rain Before Seven*, by Joyce Dennys (Dir. Michael Barry)
21 June:	*Lucretia*, by Ernita Lascelles (Dir. Reginald Tate)
5 July:	*Rich Man—Poor Man—*, by John Gliddon and G.K. Alan (Dir. Dennis Arundell)
6 September:	*Laura Garnett*, by Leslie and Sewell Stokes (Dir. Dennis Arundell)
20 September:	*Front of House*, by Charles Landstone (Dir. Ronald Shiner)

4 October:	*Time and the Hour,* by Alan Kennington and William McElwee (Dir. Godfrey Kenton)
7 October:	*The Champblays,* by Rupert Stutfield (Dir. Fred O'Donovan)
18 October:	*The Palmist,* by John Burch (Dir. Fred Groves)
22 October:	*The Servant of Two Masters,* by Carlo Goldoni (Dir. Henry Burton)
7 November:	*Poor Man's Castle,* by Mundy Whitehouse and Barbara Blackburn (Dir. A.R. Whatmore)
15 Novermber:	*Twenty Shadows,* by Dorothy Maude (Dir. Robert Young)
22 November:	*King's Pleasure,* by Jonathan Field (Dir. Michael Martin-Harvey)
6 December:	*Honour Thy Father,* by Diana Hamilton (Dir. Jack Hawkins)
20 December:	*Strange Incident,* by Clive Desmond (Dir. David Horne)
26 December:	*The Soul of Nicholas Snyders,* by Jerome K. Jerome

1937

14 January:	*Son of the Grand Eunuch,* by Albert Arlen from the French novel by Charles Pettit (Dir. Godfrey Baxter)
9 February:	*Come Out to Play,* by John Sand and Fanny Jocelyn (Dir. Edward Stirling)
21 February:	*First Night,* by Sheila Donisthorpe (Dir. A. Gardner-Davies)
7 March:	*The Heavenly Passion,* by Olga Racster and Jessica Grove (Dir. Michael Raghan)
21 March:	*Joy Will Come Back,* by Elizabeth Goudge (Dir. Muriel Pratt)
4 April:	*An Experiment in Paper Work,* by Robert Victor (Dir. Harold Clayton) *Peter Petrous,* by Robert Victor (Dir. Evan John)
8 April:	*Thou Art the Man,* by Arthur Hood (Dir. Richard Cuthbert)
16 May:	*Daughter of Ind,* by S. Fyzee Rahamin (Dir. Patrick Gover)
27 May:	*People in Love,* by Arthur Reid (Dir. Marjorie Morris)
2 June:	*Pay Day,* by B. Carlton Brown (Dir. Sydney Bland)

3 June:	*Daleby Deep*, by Horace Flather
	(Dir. Muriel Pratt)
17 June:	*The Bridge*, by Cecile Adair (Dir. Douglas Quayle)
20 June:	*The Man Who Meant Well*, by Kathleen Hewitt
	(Dir. Harold Clayton)
30 June:	*In the Best Families*, by Anita Hart and Maurice Braddell (Dir. Maurice Braddell)
4 July:	*But Not Your Heart*, by C.J. Francis
	(Dir. Wallace Geoffrey)
30 July:	*Daughter of Ind*, by S. Fyzee Rahamin
	(Dir. Patrick Gover and Ronald Giffin)
5 September:	*Van Gogh*, by Dan Burke (Dir. Fred O'Donovan)
17 September:	*Copyright Reserved*, revue by Maurice Samuel and Leslie Julian Jones (Dir. Noel Iliff)
24 October:	*Waters of Jordan*, by Christopher Steele
	(Dir. Beatrice Wilson)
31 October:	*Rendezvous*, by Raoul Ernst Weiss
	(Dir. Muriel Pratt)
21 November:	*Flying Blind*, by Pamela Kellino and James Mason
	(Dir. Roy Kellino)
28 November:	*Murder by Suggestion*, by Cecil Tailby
	(Dir. Muriel Pratt)

1938

16 January:	*Beloved*, adapted from the French of André de Chatellus by Valerie Wyngate
	(Dir. Marjorie Morris)
21 January:	*Hamlet*, by William Shakespeare (Dir. W.G. Fay)
30 January:	*But for the Grace*, by Travers Otway
	(Dir. Muriel Pratt)
13 February:	*The Second Mr. Bush*, by Stafford Dickens
	(Dir. The Author)
27 March:	*Summer for Seven*, by John McNair
	(Dir. Charles Hickman)
24 April:	*Murder Without Tears*, by Florence A. Kilpatrick
	(Dir. Sydney Monkton)
1 May:	*High Fever*, by Winifred Carter
	(Dir. G. Hamilton Gay)
5 May:	*A Star Comes Home*, by Reginald Long
	(Dir. Muriel Pratt)
15 May:	*Peace and Goodwill*, by Harold Bowen
	(Dir. Auriol Lee)

10 July:	*...And Life Burns On*, by Virginia Isham and Richard George (Dir. Milton Rosmer)
24 July:	*Mr. Mercury*, by Peter E. Rodgers (Dir. Evelyn Cecil)
25 September:	*Blind Man's Buff*, by Ernst Toller and Denis Johnston (Dir. John Fernald)
11 October:	*A Party for Christmas*, by N.C. Hunter (Dir. John Fernald)
25 October:	*Oscar Wilde*, by Leslie and Sewell Stokes

1939

26 March:	*Sons of Adam*, by Beatrix Thomson (Dir. Peter Creswell)
18 December:	*The Unveiling*, by Gwendolyn Downes; music by Victor Hely-Hutchinson (Dir. John Wyse)

1940

5 September:	*The Infernal Machine*, by Jean Cocteau (Dir. Charlotte Frances)

1942

20 May:	*Awake and Sing*, by Clifford Odets (Dir. Alec Clunes)
10 June:	*Twelfth Night*, by William Shakespeare (Dir. Alec Clunes)
15 July:	*The Swan Song*, by Anton Chekhov, translated by Constance Garnett (Dir. Alec Clunes) *The Springtime of Others*, by Jean-Jacques Bernard, translated by J. Leslie Frith (Dir. Maurice Colbourne)
26 August:	*The Proposal*, by Anton Chekhov (Dir. Alec Clunes) *Magic*, by G.K. Chesterton (Dirs. Alec Clunes and John Hanau)
6 October:	*House of Regrets*, by Peter Ustinov (Dir. Alec Clunes)
24 November:	*Maria Marten*, "by the Hon.--- (a Gentleman)" (Dir. Alec Clunes)
11 December:	*Holy Isle*, by James Bridie (Dir. Alastair Sim)
31 December:	*The Drunkard*, by W.H. Smith and a Gentleman (Dir. Harold Scott)

1943

12 January:	*She Stoops to Conquer,* by Oliver Goldsmith	
	(Dir. Dorothy Green)	
2 February:	*Androcles and the Lion,* by Bernard Shaw	
	(Dir. Alec Clunes)	
17 March:	*The Well of the Saints,* by J.M. Synge	
	(Dir. Alec Clunes)	
	Beyond, by Peter Ustinov (Dir. Alec Clunes)	
24 March:	*Don Juan in Hell,* by Bernard Shaw	
	(Dir. Alec Clunes)	
20 April:	*The Young and Lovely,* by Hugh Burden	
	(Dir. Henry Cass)	
7 May:	*The Old Foolishness,* by Paul Vincent Carroll	
	(Dir. Dennis Arundell)	
8 June:	*Days Without End,* by Eugene O'Neill	
	(Dir. Lewis Casson)	
18 June:	*The Judgement of Dr. Johnson,* by G.K. Chesterton	
	(Dir. Peter Creswell)	
13 July:	*Buster,* by Ted Willis (Dir. Eric Capon)	
2 July:	*The Constant Couple,* by George Farquhar	
	(Dir. Alec Clunes)	
29 July:	*The Rivals,* by Richard Brinsley Sheridan	
	(Dir. Noel Iliff)	
3 August:	*The Magistrate,* by Arthur Wing Pinero	
	(Dir. Alec Clunes)	
10 August:	*Misalliance,* by Bernard Shaw (Dir. Alec Clunes)	
24 August:	*The Watched Pot,* by H.H. Munro and Charles Maude	
	(Dir. Alec Clunes)	
23 November:	*The Recruiting Officer,* by George Farquhar	
	(Dir. Alec Clunes)	
9 December:	*On Life's Sunny Side,* by Helge Krog, translated by C.B. Burchardt (Dir. Catherine Lacey)	

1944

13 January:	*Don Abel Wrote a Tragedy,* by Serafin and Joaquin Alvarez Quintero, translated by Helen and Harley Granville-Barker (Dir. Denys Blakelock)
10 February:	*The Witch,* by H.Wiers-Jenssen, adapted by John Masefield (Dir. Catherine Lacey)
9 March:	*The Two Children,* by Peter Powell (Dir. Alec Clunes)
7 April:	*The Philanderer,* by Bernard Shaw (Dir. Henry Cass)

3 May:	*Doctor Without Medicine,* an English version of Molière's *Le Médecin Malgré Lui*
	Les Précieuses Ridicules, by Molière, performed in French (Dir. Paul Bonifas)
26 May:	*A Trip to Scarborough,* by Richard Brinsley Sheridan (Dir. Denys Blakelock)
22 June:	*The Sulky Fire,* by Jean-Jacques Bernard, translated by J. Leslie Frith (Dir. Claud Gurney)
20 July:	*Bird in Hand,* by John Drinkwater (Dir. Alec Clunes)
17 August:	*Mine Hostess,* by Carlo Goldoni, translated by Clifford Bax (Dir. Alec Clunes)
14 September:	*Fanny's First Play,* by Bernard Shaw (Dir. Molly Terraine)
19 October:	*The Breadwinner,* by W. Somerset Maugham (Dir. Leonard Sachs)
24 November:	*Anna Christie,* by Eugene O'Neill (Dir. Judith Furse)
26 December:	*The Critic,* by Richard Brinsley Sheridan (Dir. Judith Furse)

1945

2 February:	*The Copy,* by Helge Krog, translated by Roy Campbell (Dir. Judith Furse)
	Leonce and Lena, by Georg Buchner, translated by Geoffrey Dunlop
7 March:	*The Simpleton of the Unexpected Isles,* by Bernard Shaw (Dir. Judith Furse)
19 April:	*An Italian Straw Hat,* by Labiche and Marc-Michel; English version by Thomas Walton (Dir. George Howe)
31 May:	*The Government Inspector,* by Nikolay Gogol; English version by Guy McCrone (Dir. John Fernald)
26 June:	*L'Avare,* by Molière, performed in French
11 July:	*A Doll's House,* by Henrik Ibsen (Dir. John Fernald)
9 August:	*The Circle of Chalk,* adapted by Klabund from the Chinese; English version by James Laver (Dir. Christopher Fry)
5 September:	*Getting Married,* by Bernard Shaw (Dir. Judith Furse)
12 September:	*The Thunderbolt,* by Arthur Wing Pinero (Dir. Peter Streuli)

21 September:	*The School for Scandal,* by Richard Brinsley Sheridan (Dir. Christopher Fry)
27 September:	*The Constant Couple,* by George Farquhar (Dir. Alec Clunes)
10 October:	*Hamlet,* by William Shakespeare (Dir. Judith Furse)

1946

13 March:	*The Lady from the Sea,* by Henrik Ibsen; translated by Eleanor Marx-Aveling (Dir. Judith Furse)
18 April:	*Exercise Bowler,* by "T. Atkinson" (Peter Powell, William Fox, Torin Thatcher, Alec Clunes and W.P. Templeton) (Dir. Peter Powell)
30 April:	*Dutch Family,* by August Defresne (Dir. Peter Streuli)
29 May:	*You Won't Need the Halo,* by W.P. Templeton (Dir. Peter Streuli)
11 June:	*The Dove and the Carpenter,* by L.E. Jones (Dir. Peter Powell)
3 July:	*Don Juan in Hell,* by Bernard Shaw (Dir. Peter Powell)
16 July:	*Vicious Circle,* by Jean-Paul Sartre, translated from *Huis Clos* by Marjorie Gabain and Joan Swinstead (Dir. Peter Brook)
7 August:	*The Apple Cart,* by Bernard Shaw (Dirs. Jack Hawkins and Peter Streuli)
3 September:	*The Scheming Lieutenant; or St. Patrick's Day,* by Richard Brinsley Sheridan (Dir. Colin Chandler)
10 September:	*The Constant Wife,* by W. Somerset Maugham (Dirs. Noel Howlett and Leonard Brett)
10 October:	*On the Way,* by Helge Krog, translated by Herbert Yourelle (Dir. Beatrix Lehmann)
23 October:	*The Turn of the Screw,* adapted by Allan Turpin from the story by Henry James (Dir. Noel Willman)
6 November:	*The Rising Sun,* by Herman Heijermans, translated by Christopher St. John (Dir. Beatrix Lehmann)
20 November:	*A Phoenix Too Frequent,* by Christopher Fry (Dir. Noel Willman)
5 December:	*Fatal Curiosity,* by George Lillo (Dir. Beatrix Lehmann)

1947

1 January:	*The Master Builder,* by Henrik Ibsen (Dir. Peter Ashmore)
4 February:	*The Wise Have Not Spoken,* by Paul Vincent Carroll (Dir. Basil C. Langton)
18 February:	*Back to Methuselah,* Part I, by Bernard Shaw (Dir. Noel Willman)
19 February:	*Back to Methuselah,* Parts 2 and 3, by Bernard Shaw (Dir. Noel Willman)
25 February:	*Back to Methuselah,* Part 4, by Bernard Shaw (Dir. Noel Willman)
4 March:	*Back to Methuselah,* Part 5, by Bernard Shaw (Dir. Noel Willman)
29 April:	*Less Than Kind,* by François Mauriac, translated by Basil Bartlett (Dir. Norman Marshall)
28 May:	*Boys in Brown,* by Reginald Beckwith (Dir. Norman Marshall)
2 July:	*Maya,* by Simon Gantillon, adapted by Virginia and Frank Vernon (Dir. Norman Marshall)
7 August:	*Trapeze at the Vatican,* by Kurt Johannes Braun, version by Ashley Dukes (Dir. C. Denis Freeman)
2 September:	*Child's Play,* by Reginald Beckwith (Dir. Norman Marshall)
1 October:	*Cupid and Mars,* by Rodney Ackland and Robert G. Newton (Dir. Peter Powell)
30 October:	*Smith,* by W. Somerset Maugham (Dir. Peter Powell)
26 November:	*The Moon in the Yellow River,* by Denis Johnston (Dir. Frank Harvey)
19 December:	*Pride Shall Have a Fall,* by George Croly (Dir. Peter Powell)

1948

20 January:	*Invitation to a Voyage,* by Jean-Jacques Bernard; translated by J. Leslie Frith (Dir. Peter Powell)
11 February:	*A Comedy of Good and Evil,* by Richard Hughes (Dir. Vivienne Bennett)
10 March:	*The Lady's Not for Burning,* by Christopher Fry (Dir. Jack Hawkins)
30 March:	*Major Barbara,* by Bernard Shaw (Dir. Peter Glenville)
20 April:	*Break-Up,* by Helge Krog (Dir. Dennis Arundell)

26 May:	*Musical Chairs,* by Ronald Mackenzie
	(Dir. Peter Potter)
8 July:	*Rosmersholm,* by Henrik Ibsen (Dir. Peter Powell)
20 July:	*Too True to be Good,* by Bernard Shaw
	(Dir. Esmé Percy)
3 August:	*Tartuffe,* by Molière; translated by the Earl of Longford (Dir. Peter Powell)
9 September:	*The Cherry Orchard,* by Anton Chekhov
	(Dir. Peter Powell)
14 October:	*The Bear,* by Anton Chekhov
	(Dir. Lucie Mannheim)
	Marriage, by Gogol (Dir. Lucie Mannheim)
10 November:	*The Third Man,* by Louis Verneuil (a version of *Monsieur Lamberthier*) (Dir. Lucie Mannheim)
1 December:	*Gog and MacGog,* by James Bridie
	(Dir. Esmé Percy)

1949

4 January:	*A Pair of Spectacles,* by Sydney Grundy
	(Dir. Alec Clunes)
2 February:	*Widowers' Houses,* by Bernard Shaw
	(Dir. Esmé Percy)
24 February:	*The Unquiet Spirit,* by Jean-Jacques Bernard; translated by J. Leslie Frith (Dir. John Fernald)
22 March:	*Caroline,* by W. Somerset Maugham
	(Dir. Joan Swinstead)
19 April:	*She Stoops to Conquer,* by Oliver Goldsmith
	(Dir. Roy Rich)
18 May:	*The Male Animal,* by James Thurber and Elliott Nugent (Dir. Roy Rich)
21 June:	*The Mollusc,* by Hubert Henry Davies
	(Dir. Joan Swinstead)
3 August:	*The Schoolmistress,* by Arthur Wing Pinero
	(Dir. John Fernald)
30 August:	*The Romantic Young Lady,* by Gregorio Martinez Sierra; English version by Helen and Harley Granville-Barker (Dir. Roy Rich)
19 October:	*The Diary of a Scoundrel,* by Rodney Ackland, adapted from the original of Ostrovsky (Dir. Roy Rich)
23 November:	*Hindle Wakes,* by Stanley Houghton
	(Dir. Alec Clunes)
22 December:	*The Silver Curlew,* by Eleanor Farjeon; music by Clifton Parker (Dir. John Fernald)

1950

25 January:	*Mrs. Warren's Profession,* by Bernard Shaw
	(Dir. Roy Rich)
1 March:	*John Gabriel Borkman,* by Henrik Ibsen; English version by John Fernald and Jenny Laird
	(Dir. John Fernald)
22 March:	*The Provok'd Wife,* by Sir John Vanbrugh
	(Dir. Max Adrian)
20 April:	*Ivanov,* by Anton Chekhov; English version by J.P. Davis (Dir. John Fernald)
8 June:	*Macbeth,* by William Shakespeare
	(Dir. Alec Clunes)
5 July:	*Heartbreak House,* by Bernard Shaw
	(Dir. John Fernald)
2 August:	*The Gentle Gunman,* by Roger MacDougall
	(Dir. Roy Rich)
31 August:	*Home and Beauty,* by W. Somerset Maugham
	(Dir. Roy Rich)
19 September:	*The Mask and the Face,* by C.B. Fernald based on the comedy by Luigi Chiarelli (Dir. John Fernald)
10 October:	*Queen Elizabeth,* by Hugh Ross Williamson
	(Dir. Alec Clunes)
15 November:	*Preserving Mr. Panmure,* by Arthur Wing Pinero
	(Dir. John Fernald)
13 December:	*Lady Precious Stream,* by S.I. Hsiung
	(Dir. Roy Rich)

1951

17 January:	*Hedda Gabler,* by Henrik Ibsen; version by Edmund Gosse and William Archer (Dir. Roy Rich)
13 February:	*Spring at Marino,* by Constance Cox
	(Dir. John Fernald)
21 March:	*Intimate Relations,* by Jean Cocteau; translated by Charles Frank
26 April:	Shaw Festival, first programme:
	Great Catherine (Dir. Stephen Murray)
	How he Lied to her Husband (Dir. Stephen Murray)
	Passion, Poison, and Petrifaction (Dir. Judith Furse)
	The Admirable Bashville (Dir. Judith Furse)
16 May:	Shaw Festival, second programme:
	The Inca of Perusalem
	The Fascinating Foundling

	The Shewing-up of Blanco Posnet
	Press Cuttings
	(Dirs. Judith Furse and Stephen Murray)
20 June:	Shaw Festival, third programme:
	Augustus Does His Bit
	Village Wooing
	Annajanska, The Bolshevik Empress
	The Glimpse of Reality
	Overruled (Dirs. Roy Rich and John Fernald)
27 June:	Shaw Festival, fourth programme:
	O'Flaherty, V.C.
	The Six of Calais
	The Man of Destiny
	The Music Cure
	The Dark Lady of the Sonnets
	(Dirs. Roy Rich and John Fernald)
18 July: ·	*Poor Judas*, by Enid Bagnold (Dir. Roy Rich)
16 August:	*Right Side Up*, by C.E. Webber (Dir. Roy Rich)
5 September:	*Saint's Day*, by John Whiting
	(Dir. Stephen Murray)
28 September:	*Mrs. Dot*, by W. Somerset Maugham
	(Dir. Joan Swinstead)
30 October:	*Third Person*, by Andrew Rosenthal
	(Dir. Roy Rich)
4 December:	*The Great Adventure*, by Arnold Bennett
	(Dir. John Fernald)

1952

3 January:	*Thieves' Carnival*, by Jean Anouilh, translated by Lucienne Hill (Dir. Roy Rich)
26 February:	*To See Ourselves*, by E.M. Delafield
	(Dir. Roy Rich)
27 March:	*Uncle Vanya*, by Anton Chekhov, new version by J.P. Davis (Dir. John Fernald)
6 May:	*The Voysey Inheritance*, by Harley Granville-Barker
	(Dir. John Fernald)
4 June:	*Hobson's Choice*, by Harold Brighouse
	(Dir. Roy Rich)
9 July:	*The Way to Keep Him*, by Arthur Murphy
	(Dir. Stephen Murray)
30 July:	*In Chancery*, by Arthur Wing Pinero
	(Dir. John Fernald)

8 September:	*Don Juan in Hell,* by Bernard Shaw
	(Dir. Alec Clunes)
24 September:	*Two Loves I Have,* by Dorothy and Howard Baker
	(Dir. Roy Rich)
23 October:	*Lord Arthur Savile's Crime,* by Basil Dawson and St. John Clowes from the short story by Oscar Wilde
	(Dir. Stephen Murray)
20 November:	*The Holy Terrors,* by Jean Cocteau; English version by Edward O. Marsh (Dir. John Fernald)
19 December:	*Maria Marten,* revised and reformed by Alec Clunes
	(Dir. Alec Clunes)

1953

28 January:	*The Breadwinner,* by W. Somerset Maugham
	(Dir. Roy Rich)
26 February:	*The Father,* by August Strindberg, new version by J.P. Davis (Dir. Peter Cotes)
23 April:	*The Seagull,* by Anton Chekhov (Dir. John Fernald)
20 May:	*Second Best Bed,* by N. Richard Nash
	(Dir. John Fernald)
25 June:	*Arms and the Man,* by Bernard Shaw
	(Dir. Alec Clunes)
	The Bespoke Overcoat, by Wolf Mankowitz
	(Dir. Alec Clunes)
22 July:	*Tobias and the Angel,* by James Bridie
	(Dir. Judith Furse)
11 August:	*Dust Under Our Feet,* by Michael J. Murphy
	(Dir. Harold Goldblatt)
10 September:	*Penelope,* by W. Somerset Maugham
	(Dir. Walter Hudd)
21 October:	*Drama at Inish,* by Lennox Robinson
	(Dir. Charles Hickman)
16 December:	*A London Actress,* by Emma Litchfield
	(Dir. Charles Hickman)

1954

13 January:	*Crime and Punishment,* adapted from Dostoevsky by Gaston Baty (Dir. John Fernald)
3 February:	*The Private Secretary,* by Charles Hawtrey
	(Dir. Hugh Miller)
3 March:	*Blood Wedding,* by Frederico Garcia Lorca, translated by Richard L. O'Connell and James Graham-Lujan
	(Dir. Peter Hall)

1 April:	*The Enchanted*, by Jean Giraudoux, adapted by Maurice Valency (Dir. John Fernald)
29 April:	*The Sun Room*, by Romilly Cavan (Dir. John Fernald)
26 May:	*The Impresario from Smyrna*, by Carlo Goldoni, translated by Clifford Bax (Dir. Peter Hall)
23 June:	*Six Characters in Search of an Author*, by Luigi Pirandello, translated by Frederick May (Dir. Royston Morley)
12 July:	*Edmée*, by P.A. Bréal, performed in French (Dir. William Jacques)
1 September:	*The Diary of a Nobody*, adapted from the book by George and Weedon Grossmith by Basil Dean and Richard Blake (Dir. Basil Dean)
29 September:	*Saint Joan*, by Bernard Shaw (Dir. Michael Langham)
3 November:	*The Immoralist*, based on the book by André Gide by Ruth and Augustus Goetz (Dir. Peter Hall)
7 December:	*Never Get Out*, by Giles Cooper
15 December:	*Top Note*, devised by Antony Hopkins

1955

13 January:	*The Rules of the Game*, by Luigi Pirandello, translated by Robert Rietty and Noel Cregeen (Dir. John Fernald)
9 February:	*The Ghost Writers*, by Ted Allan (Dir. Bernard Braden)
9 March:	*The Lesson*, by Eugene Ionesco, translated by Donald Watson (Dir. Peter Hall)
	Sacrifice to the Wind, by André Obey, English version by John Whiting
30 March:	*South*, by Julien Green (Dir. Peter Hall)
4 May:	*The Midnight Family*, by Charles Dorat, translated by Gillian Winter (Dir. John Fernald)
9 June:	*Mourning Becomes Electra*, by Eugene O'Neill (Dir. Peter Hall)
3 August:	*Waiting for Godot*, by Samuel Beckett (Dir. Peter Hall)
9 September:	*The Burnt Flower Bed*, by Ugo Betti, translated by Henry Reed (Dir. Peter Hall)
8 November:	*Komuso*, by Robert Nichols (Dir. Guy Verney)
16 December:	*Listen to the Wind*, by Angela Ainley Jeans; music and lyrics by Vivian Ellis (Dir. Peter Hall)

1956

27 January:	*Darkling Child*, by W.S. Merwin in collaboration with Dido Milroy (Dir. Frith Banbury)
24 February:	*The Waltz of the Toreadors*, by Jean Anouilh, translated by Lucienne Hill (Dir. Peter Hall)
28 March:	*The Comedy of Errors*, by William Shakespeare, adapted by Lionel Harris and Robert J. McNab, music by Julian Slade (Dir. Lionel Harris)
1 May:	*Late Interlude*, a revue by Honoria Plesch, who directed
30 May:	*Off the Mainland*, by Robert Shaw (Dir. Andre van Gyseghem)
4 July:	*The Trip to Bountiful*, by Horton Foote (Dir. Alan Schneider)
15 August:	*The Young and Beautiful*, by Sally Benson (Dir. Fred Sadoff)
19 September:	*The Children's Hour*, by Lillian Hellman (Dir. Graham Evans)
6 November:	*The Bald Prima Donna*, by Eugene Ionesco, translated by Donald Watson (Dir. Peter Wood)
	The New Tenant, by Eugene Ionesco, translated by Donald Watson (Dir. Peter Wood)
20 December:	*The Ticket-of-Leave Man*, by Tom Taylor (Dir. Walter Hudd)
26 December:	*The Princess and the Swineherd*, by Nicholas Stuart Gray (Dir. Graham Evans)

1957

24 January:	*No Laughing Matter*, by Armand Salacrou, translated by Lucienne Hill (Dir. Peter Wood)
12 March:	*The Wit to Woo*, by Mervyn Peake (Dir. Peter Wood)
22 April:	*The Balcony*, by Jean Genet translated by Bernard Frechtman (Dir. Peter Zadek)
11 June:	*Time to Speak*, by Sylvia Rayman (Dir. Nancy Poultney)
27 June:	*Less Than Kind*, by Derek Monsey (Dir. Yvonne Mitchell)
31 July:	*Yerma*, by Frederico Garcia Lorca, translated by James Graham-Lugan and Richard L. O'Connell (Dir. Clifford Williams)
28 August:	*A Lonesome Road*, by Philip King and Robin Maugham (Dir. Jack Williams)

19 September:	*All Kinds of Men*, by Alex Samuels
	(Dir. Robert Mitchell)
15 October:	*The Public Prosecutor*, by Fritz Hochwälder, translated by Kitty Black (Dir. Alan Badel)
19 December:	*No Clothes for the Emperor*, by Nicholas Stuart Gray (Dir. Stuart Latham)
27 December:	*A Stranger in the Tea*, by Lilian and Edward Percy, based on Sheridan le Fanu (Dir. Jordan Lawrence)

1958

29 January:	*The Iceman Cometh*, by Eugene O'Neill
	(Dir. Peter Wood)
25 March:	*The Catalyst*, by Ronald Duncan (Dir. Phil Brown)
7 April:	*The Imperial Nightingale*, by Nicholas Stuart Gray (Dir. The Author)
1 May:	*Quaint Honour*, by Roger Gellert (Dir. Frank Dunlop)
3 June:	*Something's Burning*, by Bon Viveur (Dir. Eric Croall)
19 June:	*Templeton*, by Anthony Lock (Dir. John Gibson)
18 July:	*Noon Has No Shadows*, by Patricia Joudry (Dir. Leon Major)
20 August:	*Ariadne*, By Gabriel Marcel, translated by Rosalind Heywood (Dir. Milo Sperber)
16 September:	*Garden District*: a double bill of Tennessee Williams' *Suddenly Last Summer* and *Something Unspoken* (Dir. Herbert Machiz)
29 October:	*Garden of Loneliness*, by Gerhart Hauptmann, English version by Richard Duschinsky, who directed
27 November:	*The Devil Peter*, by Salvato Cappelli, translated by Giampiero Rolandi (Dir. Robert Peake)
26 December:	*Radio Rescue*, by Charlotte B. Chorpenning (Dir. Clifford Williams)

1959

29 January:	*Madame de...* by Jean Anouilh based on a story by Louise de Vilmorin, translated by John Whiting *Traveller Without Luggage*, by Jean Anouilh, translated by John Whiting (Dir. Peter Hall)
12 March:	*The Buskers*, by Kenneth Jupp (Dir. Toby Robertson)
14 April:	*Dark Halo*, by Sylvia Leigh (Dir. Clifford Williams)

21 May:	*Ulysses in Nighttown,* dramatised from James Joyce by Marjorie Barkentin (Dir. Burgess Meredith)
9 July:	*The Rope Dancers,* by Morton Wishengrad (Dir. Peter Cotes)
5 August:	*Clair de Lune,* by Rae Jenkins *Deutsches Haus,* by Richard Cottrell
19 August:	*Quartet for Five,* by Marc Camoletti, translated by Warren Tute (Dir. Clifford Williams)
30 December:	*The Marriage of Mr. Mississippi,* by Friedrich Durrenmatt, translated by Eric Peters and Robert Schnorr (Dir. Clifford Williams)
21 October:	*My Friend Judas,* by Andrew Sinclair (Dir. Fred Sadoff)
18 November:	*Man's Job,* by Ferdinand Bruckner, translated by Richard Duschinsky who directed
23 December:	*Beauty and the Beast,* by Nicholas Stuart Gray (Dirs. The Author and Ruth Atkinson)

1960

20 January:	*A Moon for the Misbegotten,* by Eugene O'Neill (Dir. Clifford Williams)
1 March:	*Change for the Angel,* by Bernard Kops (Dir. David de Keyser)
30 March:	*The Admiration of Life,* by Patricia Broderick (Dir. Vivian Matalon)
27 April:	*The Caretaker,* by Harold Pinter (Dir. Donald McWhinnie)
1 June:	*A Trip to the Castle,* by George Buchanan (Dir. Robert Cartland)
29 June:	*The Shepherd's Chameleon,* by Eugene Ionesco *Victims of Duty,* by Eugene Ionesco (Both dir. by Clifford Williams)
26 July:	*The Last Angle,* by Charles Lincoln (Dir. Clifford Williams)
25 August:	*The Zoo Story,* by Edward Albee (Dir. Henry Kaplan) *This Property is Condemned,* by Tenessee Williams (Dir. Donald Howarth)
29 September:	*Naked Island,* by Russell Braddon (Dir. Edward Burnham)
2 November:	*This Way to the Tomb,* by Ronald Duncan with music by Benjamin Britten (Dir. Frank Dunlop)

| 21 December: | *The Imperial Nightingale,* by Nicholas Stuart Gray |
| | (Dir. The Author) |

1961

18 January:	*Three---*
	Lunch Hour, by John Mortimer
	The Form, by N.F. Simpson
	A Slight Ache, by Harold Pinter
	(Dir. Donald McWhinnie)
15 February:	*Stop it, Whoever You Are,* by Henry Livings
	(Dir. Vida Hope)
21 March:	*You in Your Small Corner,* by Barry Reckord
	(Dir. John Bird)
17 April:	*Breakfast for One,* by James Doran
	(Dir. Silvio Narizzant)
18 May:	*Three Posts on the Square,* by Leo Heaps
	(Dir. David Giles)
13 June:	*Tresper Revolution,* by George Buchanan
	(Dir. Ian Curteis)
25 June:	*Deathwatch,* by Genet, translated by Bernard Frechtman
	The Splits, by Georges Neveux, translated by Edward Owen Marsh (Dir. Ronald Hayman)
10 July:	*The Kreutzer Sonata,* based on Tolstoy's story, translated by Aylmer Maude (Dir. Louis Lentin)
19 September:	*Finder's Keepers,* by Richard Easton
	(Dir. Robert Cartland)
19 October:	*Ducks and Lovers,* by Murray Schisgal
	(Dir. Philip Saville)
15 November:	*The Cupboard,* by Ray Rigby (Dir. Basil Ashmore)
14 December:	*4 to the Bar,* (Dir. Charles Ross)
21 December:	*The Circus Adventure,* by James Ambrose Brown
	(Dir. Caryl Jenner)

1962

16 January:	*The Knacker's Yard,* by Johnny Speight
	(Dir. Alan Simpson)
16 February:	*Twists,* by Steven Vinaver, with music by Carl Davis
	(Dir. The Author)
13 March:	*Everything in the Garden,* by Giles Cooper
	(Dir. Donald McWhinnie)
12 April:	*Nil Carborundum,* by Henry Livings
	(Dir. Anthony Page)

9 May:	*The Lower Depths,* by Maxim Gorki, adapted by Derek Marlowe from Moura Budberg's translation (Dir. Toby Robertson)
7 June:	*Afore Night Come,* by David Rudkin (Dir. Clifford Williams)
4 July:	*Women Beware Women,* by Thomas Middleton (Dir. Anthony Page)
31 July:	*The Empire Builders,* by Boris Vian, translated from the French by Simon Watson Taylor (Dir. David Jones)
29 August:	*Infanticide in the House of Fred Ginger,* by Fred Watson (Dir. William Gaskill)
2 October:	*Doctors of Philosophy,* by Muriel Spark (Dir. Donald McWhinnie)
16 October:	*End of Day,* by Samuel Beckett, with music by Miles Davis, a one-man show by Jack McGowran (Dir. Donald McWhinnie)
20 November:	*A Cheap Bunch of Nice Flowers,* by Edna O'Brien (Dir. Desmond T. O'Donovan)
19 December:	*Amelia's African Adventure,* by James Ambrose Brown (Dir. Caryl Jenner)
26 December:	*3 at Nine,* (Dir. Eleanor Fazan)

1963

23 January:	*Next Time I'll Sing to You,* by James Saunders (Dir. Shirley Butler)
20 February:	*The Blood Knot,* by Athol Fugard (Dir. John Berry)
20 March:	*Divorce à la Carte,* by Victorien Sardou and Emile de Najac, adapted by Diane Hart and Louis Manson (Dir. Frank Hauser)
24 April:	*Luv,* by Murray Schisgal (Dir. Ted Kotcheff)
6 June:	*Where Angels Fear to Tread,* by Elizabeth Hart, based on the novel by E.M. Forster (Dir. Glen Byam Shaw)
22 August:	*Afternoon Men,* by Riccardo Aragno, based on the novel by Anthony Powell (Dir. Roger Graaf)
18 September:	*The Lover* *The Dwarfs,* by Harold Pinter (Dir. The Author)
9 October:	*Four and a Tanner,* by Tony Tanner; additional material by Donald Webster and music by Neville McGrah (Dir. Tony Tanner)

16 October:	*Cockade*—
	Prisoner and Escort,
	John Thomas,
	Spare, by Charles Wood (Dir. Patrick Dromgoole)
13 November:	*Poor Bitos,* by Jean Anouilh, translated by Lucienne Hill (Dir. Shirley Butler)
18 December:	*The Panther and the Unicorn,* by Oliver Jennings (Dir. Caryl Jenner)
20 December:	*Mango-Leaf Magic,* by James Ambrose Brown (Dir. Caryl Jenner)
23 December:	*Cindy-Ella,* by Caryl Brahms and Ned Sherrin, with additional music by Peter Knight and Ron Grainer (Dir. Colin Graham)

1964

21 January:	*The Brontës,* a dramatic portrait of Charlotte, Emily and Ann Brontë, arranged and adapted by Margaret Webster
12 February:	*Hedda Gabler,* by Henrik Ibsen, translated by Max Faber (Dir. Minos Volanakis)
18 March:	*The Formation Dancers,* by Frank Marcus (Dir. Clive Donner)
30 March:	*The Three Wishes,* by James Ambrose Brown (Dir. Caryl Jenner)
14 April:	*The Subtopians,* by Terence Frisby (Dir. The Author)
6 May:	*Entertaining Mr. Sloane,* by Joe Orton (Dir. Patrick Dromgoole)
1 July:	*Edward the Second,* by Christopher Marlowe (Dir. Clive Perry)
6 August:	*Mr. Whatnot,* by Alan Ayckbourn (Dir. Warren Jenkins)
1 September:	*The Striplings,* by Nina Warner Hooke (Dir. Joan Knight)
29 September:	*Games,* two plays by Fred Sadoff (Dir. The Author)
22 October:	*The Love Game,* by Marcel Achard, adapted by Willis Hall and translated by Tamara Lo (Dir. Patrick Dromgoole)
25 October:	*Two Pails of Water,* by A.E. Greidanus, translated by Bill Honeywood (Dir. Matyelok Gibbs)
16 November:	*In White America,* by Martin B. Duberman (Dir. Peter Coe)

21 December:	*The Tingalary Bird,* by Mary Melwood
	(Dir. Caryl Jenner)
23 December:	*Lady Audley's Secret,* by C.H. Hazlewood, adapted from the novel by M.E. Braddon
	(Dir. Caryl Jenner)

1965

13 February:	*The Dancing Donkey,* by Eric Vos, translated by Bill Honeywood (Dir. Matyelok Gibbs)
17 February:	*Miss Julie,* by August Strindberg, translated by Elizabeth Sprigge (Dir. Hana Pravda)
	Crawling Arnold, by Jules Feiffer
	(Dir. Charles Marowitz)
17 March:	*Kindly Monkeys,* by Milton Hood Ward
	(Dir. Krishna Shah)
20 March:	*The Golden Shaft,* by Edwin Thornley
	The Caliph's Minstrel, by Constance Cox
	(Dir. Caryl Jenner)
14 April:	*The Game as Played,* by Leon Griffiths
	(Dir. David Greene)
19 April:	*The Man who Killed Time,* by Arthur Fauquez, translated by Margaret Leona and Marie-Louise Roelants (Dir. Caryl Jenner)
8 June:	*Paint Myself Black,* by Claudine Henry
	(Dir. Peter Cotes)
29 June:	*Patent Pending,* by Wim van Leer (Dir. John Brittany)
2 September:	*Green Julia,* by Paul Abelman
	(Dir. George Mully)
21 September:	*Happy Days are Here Again,* by Samuel Beckett
	(Dir. Charles Marowitz)
25 September:	*The Art of Samuel Beckett,* selected by John Calder, who directed
6 November:	*The Strange Machine of Professor Filarsky,* by Eric Vos, translated by Bill Honeywood (Dir. Caryl Jenner)
23 November:	*Man and Superman,* by Bernard Shaw
	(Dir. Philip Wiseman)
20 December:	*The Wappy Water Bus,* by Marged Smith
	(Dir. Caryl Jenner)

1966

| 5 January: | *How's the World Treating You?* by Roger Milner, with musical effects by Ian Kellen (Dir. Philip Grout) |

16 February:	*A Smashing Day*, by Alan Plater, with music by Ben Kingsley and Robert Powell (Dir. Brian Epstein)
19 February:	*The Pied Piper*, by W.R. Latham
	The Trial of Croaker Raven, by W.R. Latham
	(Dir. Caryl Jenner)
18 May:	*The Three Musketeers*, a musical adaptation from Alexandre Dumas by Bruce Lacey and the Alberts
	(Dir. Eleanor Fazan)
22 May:	*The Downsideup Man*, by Ian Whybrow
	(Dir. Caryl Jenner)
14 June:	*Pride and Prejudice*, by James Liggatt and Robert Sheaf from the novel by Jane Austen
	(Dir. David Phethean)
7 July:	*The Waiting Game*, by Leonard Samson
	(Dir. Hugh Goldie)
3 August:	*The Thunderbolt*, by A.W. Pinero, adapted by Brian Oulton (Dir. Jordan Lawrence)
30 August:	*Early One Morning*, by Glyn Jones
	(Dir. David Poulson)
10 September:	*The Heartless Princess*, by Franklyn Black
	(Dir. Caryl Jenner)
26 September:	*A Matter of Choice*, with original material by Hugh Hastings and Alan Reeve-Jones
	(Dirs. Patrick Desmond and Ellen Pollock)
4 October:	*The Swallows*, by Roland Dubillard
	(Dir. Don Taylor)
22 November:	*This and That*, revue compiled and directed by Jimmy and Gilda Perry (Dir. by the compilers)
22 December:	*The Thirteen Clocks*, by James Thurber, adapted by Frank Lowe with music by Robert Gallico
	(Dir. Caryl Jenner)

1967

9 January:	*The Six O'Clock Holiday Show*, by Larry Adler and Shirley Abicair (Dir. George Mully)
16 January:	*The Experiment*, by David Halliwell and David Calderisi, who directed.
14 February:	*Will Somebody Please Say Something*, by David Baxter with music by David Allen (Dir. David Calderisi)
27 March:	*The Lord of the Amber Mountain*, by Derek Lamos
	(Dir. Caryl Jenner)
20 May:	*The Kennington Lion*, by Vivienne Pye
	(Dir. Caryl Jenner)

27 June:	*Mourning Becomes Electra*, by Eugene O'Neill
	(Dir. Gordon Macdougall)
16 September:	*Thieves on Board*, by Per Edstrom, translated by Patricia Crampton (Dir. Ursula Jones)
21 September:	*One in the Eye*, by John Dalby and Denise Hirst (Dir. Laurier Lister)
12 October:	*Buroctopus*, by Rene Tholy, translated by Jack Beeching
	Quotidians, by Rene Tholy, translated by Jack Beeching (Dir. Caryl Jenner)
31 October:	*Red Noses for Me*, a one-man show, by Charles Lewsen
4 November:	*The Batterpool Business*, by Diana Wynne Jones (Dir. Caryl Jenner)
9 November:	*The Laundry*, by David Guerdon, adapted by Howard Richardson (Dir. Sandor Eles)
18 December:	*The Snow Queen*, by Noel Langley (Dir. Caryl Jenner)
21 December:	*The Royal Pardon*, by John Arden and Margaretta D'Arcy (Dir. Christopher Brock)

1968

22 February:	*The Farce of Death Who Almost Died*, by Michel Ghelderode, translated by George Hauger
	The Proposal, by Anton Chekhov, translated by Ronald Hingley,
	Passion, Poison, and Petrifaction, by Bernard Shaw (Dirs. Caryl Jenner and Matyelok Gibbs)
20 March:	*The Outcry*, by Henry James (Dir. Campbell Allen)
14 May:	*Medea*, by Euripides
	Epitafios, by Iannis Ritsos, translated by George Thomson (Dir. Walter Eysselinck)
18 May:	*The Royal Astrologers*, by Willis Hall (Dir. Matyelok Gibbs)
21 May:	*Electra*, by Sophocles,
	Antigone, by Sophocles, English text by George Valamvanos (Dir. Walter Eysselinck)
5 June:	*The Foundations*, by John Galsworthy (Dir. Campbell Allen)
3 August:	*The Rasputin Show*, by Michael Almaz (Dir. Chris Park)
8 August:	*The Arabian Nights*, by Richard Gill, who directed

18 September:	*Viva Viva!* translated from Machiavelli by Ian Lindsay; music by William Thacker and Trevor T. Smith (Dir. Ian Lindsay)
17 October:	*Times Are Getting Hard Boys,* by Keith Darvill, who directed
20 October:	*Johnny So Long,* by Vivienne C. Welburn, music by Julian Silverman (Dir. Celia Fuchs)
13 November:	*There Was a Man,* one-man show with John Cairney as Robert Burns, written by Thomas Wright (Dir. Dennis Ramsden)
16 December:	*The Prince, the Wolf, and the Firebird,* by Jackson Lacey (Dir. Caryl Jenner)

1969

15 February:	*The King's Things,* by Diane Wynne-Jones (Dir. Conrad Asquith)
25 February:	*The Trojan Women,* by Euripides *Agamemnon,* by Aeschylus
5 April:	*The Pobble Who Lost His Toes,* by Wilf Harvey, suggested by Edward Lear's Nonsense Songs and Stories (Dir. Caryl Jenner)
3 June:	*Etc...* by Michael Armstrong, musical arrangments by John Fiddy (Dir. Michael Armstrong)
29 June:	*The Last Chance Saloon,* by Andy Robinson, music by Judy Stewart (Dir. Joel Swick)
8 July:	*Woyzeck,* by George Büchner, translated by Ted Hoffman (Dir. Joel Swick)
19 August:	*Shirley Abicair's Evening* (Dir. Victor Spinetti)
20 September:	*Amaluk and Pabblebye,* by Colin Shaw (Dir. Caryl Jenner)
23 September:	*The Slapstick Angels,* by Alberto Perrini; English version by Robert Rietty and John Wardale (Dir. Caryl Jenner)

1970

28 January:	*Their Majesties' Delight,* by Peter Forest
11 February:	*One Is One,* one-man performance by Julian Chagrin
5 May:	*Meanwhile Back in Sparta...* by Manthos Crispis, adapted by Roland Miller and Terry Palmer from a translation by Mark Ogilvy-Grant (Dir. Terry Palmer)

15 June:	*A Man for All Occasions,* a one-man play (Bill Maynard as Charles Dickens) devised and compiled by Michael Darlow and Christine Fox
18 August:	*The Legend of the Ice Dragon,* by Richard Gill (Dir. The Author)
7 November:	*The Terrible Fisk Machine,* by Diana Wynne Jones (Dir. Caryl Jenner)
10 November:	*Cocky:* a one-man show (Russell Hunter as Henry, Lord Cockburn), by Jack Ronder (Production assistance by Victor Spinetti)

1971

11 May:	*Under Milk Wood,* by Dylan Thomas (Dir. Malcolm Taylor)
8 June:	*Albert* and *Virginia,* two plays by Richard Harris (Dir. Malcolm Taylor)
30 November:	*Mother Adam,* by Charles Dyer (Dir. The Author)

1972

| 2 May: | *Who Thought It?* by Edward Petherbridge |
| 31 May: | *Nobody Loves Wednesday,* by Allan Weiss (Dir. Malcolm Taylor) |

1973

| 14 February: | *Mahler,* by Maurice Rowdon   (Dir. Peter Watson) |

1974

| 23 May: | *Off the Peg,* by Victor Spinetti and Gordon Deighton (Dir. Victor Spinetti) |

1975

| 17 April: | *Kennedy's Children,* by Robert Patrick (Dir. Clive Donner) |

1976

| 16 June: | *Dirty Linen* and *New-found-land,* by Tom Stoppard (Dir. Ed Berman) |

1981

| 10 September: | *Macready!* a one-man show by Frank Barrie |

APPENDIX 2

We are indebted to the Unicorn Theatre for this list of its productions since 1956.

1956
The Adventures of Master Luck

1958–9
The Astonishing Adventures of Pang, by Wilfred Harvey (New Shakespeare Theatre, Liverpool)
The Wappy Waterbus
There Was Once This Man
Fly Catcher, by Wilfred Harvey
The Tunnel
Featherton, by Wilfred Harvey
The Happy Journey, by Thornton Wilder

1961
The Coral King

1963
Panther and Unicorn

1964
The Three Wishes
Lady Audley's Secret

1965
The Downsideup Man, by Ian E. Whybrow
Swords across the Mountains

1966
The Land of Green Ginger
Circus Adventure, by James Ambrose Brown

1967
The Magical Journey of James

The Batterpool Business, by Diana Wynne-Jones
Thieves on Board
Amelia's African Adventure, by James Ambrose Brown
The Bird, the Mouse and the Sausage, by Wilfred Harvey
The Kennington Lion, by Vivien Pye
The Man Who Killed Time
Lord of the Amber Mountains
Mr. Punch at Home, by Wilfred Harvey
The Royal Pardon, by John Arden and Margeretta D'Arcy
The Thirteen Clocks

1968
The Puppet Prince, by Alan Cullen
Johnny Moonbeam and the Silver Arrow, by Joseph Golden
Parafinalia, by Ken Campbell
Henry Mouse, by Roberta Dolby
The Royal Astrologers
The Snow Queen, by Noel Langley
Little King, Big King

1969
Snip, Snap Snorum; the Party that was just in Time
Amaluk and the Pabblebye/Slapstick Angels, by Robin Shaw
The Dragon's Grandmother/Swindle, by Marged Smith
The Tingalary Bird, by Mary Mellwood
The Pobble who Lost his Toes, adapted by Wilfred Harvey
The King's Things, by Diana Wynne-Jones
Parafinalia, by Ken Campbell
The Magic Forest
The Prince, the Wolf and the Firebird, by Jackson Lacey

1970
The Terrible Fish Machine, by Diana Wynne-Jones
Mr. Punch at Home, by Wilfred Harvey
The Gentle Knight, by Willis Hall/*The Golden Goose/No Talking*, by Olwen Wymark
The Flowers Shall Have a New Master, by Gregory Marshall
An Easter Egg
Wraggle Taggle Winger, by Marged Smith
The Frog Princess and the Witch
Hans who Would Not Tie his Shoelaces, by M. Randall
The Island that was Far Away, by Caryl Jenner
The Flight and the Princes, by Jackson Lacey

1971
Swag, by John Boland
Triple Bill
Gorm, by Victoria Ireland
The Disappearing Spell, by Christopher Broz
The Tale of the Red Dragon, by Alfred Bradley
The Uncomfortable Queen
Conn and the Conquerors of Space, by Bill Morrison
The Prince and the Hengirl
The Secret under the Stairs, by Gregory Marshall

1972
Thanks to Parkinson
Mrs. Princess, by Tony Godel/*The Coming of Kings*, by Ted Hughes/*What about the Crocodile*, by Madeleine Southeby
Pandemolium, by David Fisher
Puppets and Shadows
Magic for the Million, by Margaret Gibbs
Dragonless, by Brian Hales
Ships and Sealing Wax/Witch Grumpus, by Patric Campbell
Gottle, by John Boland
Tam and Cam, by Katie Hounsel-Robert/*Surprise II*
The Disappearing Spell
The Extraordinary Case of Kipper and the Cafe, by Gregory Marshall

1973
Old King Cole, by Ken Campbell (dir. Matyelok Gibbs and Ursula Jones)
Meet Mr. McIvor, by Peter Roche
Mr. Ive's Magic Punch and July Show, by John Grillo
Chinigchinich, by Olwen Wymark/*You'll Never Guess*, by Ann Jellicoe (dir. by Matyelok Gibbs)
The Hedgehog and the Hare
The Mooncusser's Daughter, by Joan Aiken
The Doomsday Buttons, by Brian Hayes
The Prince, the Wolf and the Firebird, by Jackson Lacey

1974
How We Held the Square, by David Cregan (dir. Philip Hedley)
Momotara, the Peach Boy
Five Minutes to Morning, by Mary Mellwood
Burglars/Pongo Plays, by David Rudkin and Henry Livings
The Bolting Sisters, by Olwen Wymark

Gurney and the Mysterious Machine, by David Fisher
The King and the Shirt
Jupiter 13, by Christopher Martin/*The Dragon's Grandmother,* by M. Smith
The Rainbow Robbery, by Sconlar Anderson/*Daniel Warmwell,* by M. Smith
Cinderella, by Henry Livings

1975
Orlando the Marmalade Cat Buys a Cottage, by William Corbett (dir. Ursula Jones)
The Golden Samurai, by Geoffrey Case (dir. Nicholas Barter)
Venus and Superkid, by Roland Case (dir. Chris Parr)
The Lion and the Unicorn Rumpus, by Marged Smith (dir. Ursula Jones)
Starters, by Olwen Wymark (dir. the author)
Wintherthing, by Joan Aiken (dir. Ursula Jones)
The Hour of the Werewolf, by Brian Hayles
Jack and the Beanstalk, by Henry Livings (dir. Matyelok Gibbs)

1976
Lucifer's Fair, by David Pinner (dir. Nicholas Barter)
Tales of the Impecunious Hero, by Charles Phillips
Orlando's Camping Holiday, by William Corbett (dir. Ursula Jones)
Jump, by Ken Whitmore (dir. Nicholas Barter)
Curse of the Labryrinth, by Brian Hales (dir. Matyelok Gibbs)
Two Jelliplays and a Pongo (A Good Thing and a Bad Thing/Clever Elsie/ Smiling John, Silent Peter, Daft Sam), by Ann Jellicoe and Henry Livings (dir. Nicholas Barter)
School for Clowns, by Friedrich Waelcher, translated by Ken Campbell/ *Beauty and the Beast,* by Nicholas Stuart Gray

1977
Street, by Joan Aiken (dir. Nicholas Barter)
Lizzie Dripping and the Witch, by Helen Cresswell (dir. Ursula Jones)
The Lion and Unicorn Rumpus II, by Marged Smith (dir. Ursula Jones)
Tintin's Great American Adventure, by Geoffrey Case (dir. Nicholas Barter)

1978
The White Deer, by Adrian Mitchell (dir. Ursula Jones)

Did the Spacemen Sing on the Moon, by Penny Casdagli and Ilona Sekacz (dir. Nicholas Barter)
The Blue Monster, by Carlo Gozzi, adapted by Roy Kift (dir. Nicholas Barter)
The Lion and the Unicorn Hullaballoo, by Marged Smith (dir. Nicholas Barter)
The Magic Cabbage
The Incredible Adventures of Johnny Banger, by Chris Langham (dir. Nicholas Barter)

1979
Things that Go Bump in the Night/Max and Milli, by Volker Ludwig (dir. Rod Lewis)
The Revenge of the Samurai, by Geoffrey Case (dir. Nicholas Barter)
Robinson Barleywater and the Desert Island Disco Show, by Stan Hay (dir. Nicholas Barter)
Baby Jones and the Great Art Robbery, by Gregory Marshall (dir. Sue Birtwhistle)
Gulliver's Travels, by David Illingworth (dir. Nicholas Barter)
Stop Thief! by Gregory Marshall (dir. Ursula Jones)

1980
The Dazzling Doobrywangle Dodge, by Tony Wredden and Rod Lewis (dir. Nicholas Barter)
Sadko and the Fish with Fins of Gold, by Hugh Trethowan and Juliet Dessaily (dir. Nicholas Barter)
Witch Way to the Ball, by Jackson Lacey (dir. Rod Lewis)
The Astounding Adventures of Tom Thumb or Barley Bungalore, by Henry Livings (dir. Caroline Eves)

1981
Magic Grandad, translated by Roy Kift (dir. Rod Lewis)
Sounds Like Spring, by Penny Casdagli (dir. Tony Wreddon)
Ramshackle Company, by Susan Hill (dir. Nicholas Barter)
Silent Guns, by Roger Watkins (dir. Tony Wredden)
Beowulf the Dragon Slayer, adapted by Christopher Sandford (dir. Nicholas Barter)
Meg and Mog Show, by David Wood (dir. Tony Wredden)
Who's King of the Castle, by Vicky Ireland (dir. Nicholas Barter)
Picture It! by Penny Casdagli (dir. Tony Wredden)

INDEX